Brown
Bag
Ideas From
Many Cultures

TAWA KACHINA (SUN KACHINA).

Brown Bag Ideas From Many Cultures

Irene Tejada

DAVIS PUBLICATIONS, INC.

WORCESTER, MASSACHUSETTS

DEDICATION

I DEDICATE THIS BOOK TO MY MOTHER, KATHERINE REBECCA. THROUGH HARD WORK AND PERSEVERANCE DURING THE DEPRESSION YEARS, MOTHER PROVIDED THE WHEREWITHAL FOR MY SISTER IONE, MY BROTHER CHARLES AND ME TO COMPLETE OUR EDUCATION AT THE UNIVERSITY OF MICHIGAN, WITH GRADUATE DEGREES IN EACH OF OUR CHOSEN FIELDS. THANKS MOM!

COPYRIGHT 1993

DAVIS PUBLICATIONS, INC.
WORCESTER, MA. U.S.A.

EDITOR: MARTHA SIEGEL
DESIGN: KAREN DURLACH

PRINTED IN KOREA
LIBRARY OF CONGRESS CATALOG CARD NUMBER: 92-073932
ISBN 87192-247-9
10 9 8 7 6 5 4 3 2 1

Brown Bag Ideas From Many Cultures

CONTENTS

INTRODUCTION   2

AFRICA

GHANAIAN ADINKRA CLOTH   6

BARK CLOTH   11

FANS   14

TRIBAL BEADS   19

LEATHER SHIELDS   23

DASHIKIS   27

ETHIOPIAN MAGIC SCROLLS   30

NORTH AMERICAN
WOODLAND INDIAN
BEADED VEST.

ASIA AND
THE MIDDLE EAST

INDIAN SHISHA MIRROR VESTS   36
JAVANESE SHADOW PUPPETS   40
JAPANESE DECORATIVE PAPER   47
ISRAELI MARBLE MOSAICS   52

EUROPE

ENGLISH KNIGHTS' SHIELDS   58
BELORUSSIAN STRAW PLAQUES   63
POLISH PAPER CUTS   66

FLORA AND FAUNA
FOLK PAINTING,
MEXICO.

MEXICO and THE UNITED STATES

MEXICAN AMATE PAPER IMAGES 70

MEXICAN FOLK PAINTING 74

MEXICAN SERAPES 78

MEXICAN NEARIKAS 81

COLONIAL HEX SIGN QUILTS 84

NATIVE AMERICA

MOCCASINS 90

PARFLECHE 94

SHIELDS 98

RAWHIDE VESTS 102

KACHINAS 106

SCROLLS 110

THUNDERBIRD RUGS 114

BONE BREASTPLATES 119

PAINTED BUFFALO ROBES 124

NORTH AMERICAN PLAINS INDIAN PARFLECHE.

POLYNESIA

ABORIGINAL BARK PAINTINGS 130

HAWAIIAN TAPA CLOTH 134

INTRODUCTION

YARN PAINTING BY RAMÓN MEDINA SILVA, MEXICO.

The more we know about a culture, the more we appreciate and respect its people. One way of learning about a culture is by studying its art. Art objects are often unique reflections of a culture's people. This uniqueness is strongly influenced by the local environment and the resources near at hand: straw, wood, bark, bamboo, cornhusks and leather, for example.

This book is designed to provide parents and teachers with a series of ethnic art activities for young people. The projects require few art materials and use many items found in the home, especially brown paper bags. Native craftspeople use indigenous materials that are, for us, unobtainable or too expensive, or difficult for young children to use. Other materials have been substituted to simulate the authentic items. For example, treated brown paper bags have been

SUBSTITUTED FOR LEATHER, BARK AND FABRIC. IT IS IMPORTANT FOR STUDENTS TO UNDERSTAND THAT THEY ARE NOT WORKING WITH THE REAL MATERIALS. THEY ARE USING SUBSTITUTE MATERIALS AS A WAY TO LEARN HOW AND WHY THE ORIGINAL OBJECTS ARE MADE.

IT IS ALSO IMPORTANT TO CONSIDER THE HISTORY OF ANY OBJECT THAT IS SIMULATED. THIS PROVIDES STUDENTS WITH A KNOWLEDGE OF WHERE AND WHY THE ORIGINAL OBJECTS WERE MADE, AND WHAT MATERIALS WERE USED TO FASHION THEM. THIS INFORMATION SHOULD BE ACCOMPANIED BY EXAMPLES OR PICTURES OF THE AUTHENTIC ITEMS WHENEVER POSSIBLE.

STUDENTS SHOULD BE ENCOURAGED TO USE SYMBOLS AND COLORS IN THEIR DESIGNS THAT HAVE SPECIAL MEANING FOR THEM, JUST AS THE ETHNIC DESIGNS HAVE MEANING TO THE ORIGINAL CRAFTSPEOPLE.

ART REFLECTS BOTH TRADITION AND INNOVATION. IN THE PAST, ARTISTS WERE KNOWN AND IDENTIFIED AS PART OF THEIR PARTICULAR COMMUNITY OF CRAFTSPEOPLE. THEIR ART WAS COMMISSIONED BY PRIESTS AND KINGS, OR WAS MADE FOR PERSONAL USE. TODAY, ARTISTS ARE KNOWN BY NAME, AS INDIVIDUALS. IN MANY INSTANCES, ART IS COMMISSIONED BY LOCAL GOVERNMENTS AND ART COLLECTORS. IN OTHER CASES, ART IS MADE TO SATISFY THE CREATIVE URGES AND EXPRESSIVE DESIRES OF THE ARTIST. ART OBJECTS ARE OFTEN MADE FOR SALE IN GALLERIES AND LOCAL STORES. THEY ARE CREATED FOR BOTH NATIVE AND FOREIGN AUDIENCES. IN SOME AREAS, COOPERATIVES ARE FORMED WHERE ART IS PRODUCED PRIMARILY TO BE SOLD TO THE TOURIST MARKET.

TODAY, SOME ARTISTS CONTINUE TRADITIONAL DESIGNS AND TECHNIQUES WITH FEW INNOVATIONS. OTHERS UTILIZE NEW TECHNIQUES AND ORIGINAL DESIGNS WITH TRADITIONAL MATERIALS. BY STUDYING EACH, WE CAN LEARN A GREAT DEAL ABOUT TRADITION AND INNOVATION IN ART FROM AROUND THE WORLD.

TRADE BEADS FROM AFRICA.

AFRICA

GHANAIAN ADINKRA CLOTH   6

BARK CLOTH   11

FANS   14

TRIBAL BEADS   19

LEATHER SHIELDS   23

DASHIKIS   27

ETHIOPIAN MAGIC SCROLLS   30

GHANAIAN ADINKRA CLOTH

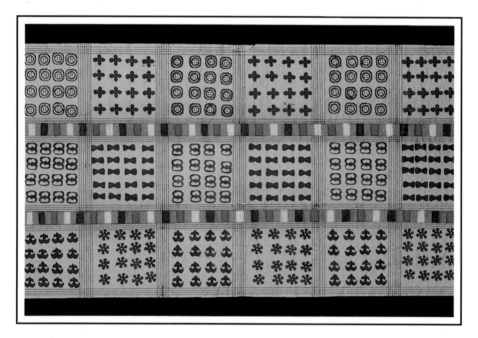

ADINKRA CLOTH IS A TYPE OF DECORATED FABRIC MADE IN GHANA, WEST AFRICA. THE WORD "ADINKRA" MEANS GOODBYE. ORIGINALLY, THE CLOTH WAS WORN EXCLUSIVELY DURING FUNERAL CEREMONIES, AND THE DESIGNS WERE PRINTED ON BROWN, BLACK OR BLUE FABRIC. ADINKRA CLOTH IS NO LONGER RESTRICTED TO PERIODS OF GRIEF. IT IS NOW A FORM OF DRESS FOR MANY IMPORTANT, DIVERSE OCCASIONS, AND THE BACKGROUND COLORS ARE BRIGHT AND COLORFUL.

THE DESIGNS STAMPED ON THE CLOTH EACH HAVE A SPECIAL MEANING. SOME MAY REPRESENT A PROVERB, WHILE OTHERS HAVE HISTORICAL OR MAGICAL SIGNIFICANCE. STILL OTHERS TRANSMIT MESSAGES CONCERNING THE WEARER OF THE GARMENT.

THE STAMPS ARE CARVED IN SMALL SECTIONS OF THE CALABASH, A GOURD THAT IS SIMILAR IN APPEARANCE TO THE GOURDS GROWN IN NORTH AMERICA. THE CALABASH GROWS

ON TROPICAL TREES. OUR GOURDS GROW ON TENDRIL-BEARING VINES. THE CALABASH HAS A THICK SHELL THAT WITHSTANDS CARVING. HANDLES OF SPLIT BAMBOO, FASHIONED LIKE A TRIPOD, ARE ATTACHED TO THE BACK OF THE CARVED CALABASH.

THE DYE IN WHICH THE STAMPS ARE PRESSED IS MADE FROM THE BARK OF THE BADIE TREE. THE BARK IS PEELED FROM THE TREE, SOAKED, POUNDED AND BOILED IN FIVE-GALLON TINS OF WATER FOR ABOUT A WEEK. DURING THE LAST FEW DAYS OF BOILING, IRON ORE IS ADDED TO THE DYE TO GIVE IT A BLACK COLOR. ONLY ONE-HALF GALLON OF LIQUID REMAINS FROM THE ORIGINAL FIVE GALLONS. LATER, AN EGG WHITE IS ADDED TO ACHIEVE A GLOSSY EFFECT (THE SAME EFFECT AS FROM COATING THE TOP OF BREAD AND PASTRY WITH EGG).

THE CLOTH USED FOR PRINTING IS MADE OF LONG STRIPS OF FABRIC THAT ARE SEWN TOGETHER WITH BRIGHTLY COLORED THREAD. THE STRIPS ARE STRETCHED TAUTLY OVER A WOODEN BOARD THAT IS PROTECTED WITH A STRAW MAT COVERING. PARALLEL LINES, MADE WITH A CARVED WOODEN COMB DIPPED IN DYE, DIVIDE THE STRIPS INTO SECTIONS. THE DESIGNS ARE THEN STAMPED WITHIN THE SECTIONS OF THE CLOTH.

IN THE VILLAGES WHERE ADINKRA FABRIC IS MADE, PEOPLE SPECIALIZE IN DIFFERENT PARTS OF ITS PRODUCTION. ONE PERSON CUTS A DESIGN FROM THE CALABASH, ANOTHER PREPARES THE DYE, OTHERS (USUALLY CHILDREN) EMBROIDER THE STRIPS TOGETHER, AND A PRINTER STAMPS THE DESIGN ON THE FABRIC.

THE FABRIC IS DRIED IN THE SUN. IT TAKES ABOUT ONE YEAR FOR THE DYE TO SET BEFORE THE FABRIC CAN BE WASHED.

BROWN BAG IDEA

MATERIALS AND TOOLS

LARGE, PLAIN BROWN PAPER BAG

ONE OR TWO SMALL POTATOES

BLACK TEMPERA PAINT

BLACK FELT-TIPPED PEN

CRAYONS AND PENCIL

SMALL DISH WITH SPONGE

PARING KNIFE OR SHARPENED TONGUE DEPRESSOR

SCISSORS

SINK OR LARGE BOWL OF WATER

RULER

DIRECTIONS

1. GIVE THE PAPER BAG A CLOTH-LIKE TEXTURE BY SOAKING IT IN WATER FOR ABOUT TEN MINUTES. THIS LOOSENS THE GLUED SEAMS.

2. OPEN THE BAG AND CAREFULLY SQUEEZE OUT THE EXCESS WATER.

3. GENTLY SPREAD OUT THE BAG ON NEWSPAPER TO DRY. SOAKING AND CRUSHING THE PAPER, THEN SQUEEZING OUT THE WATER, WILL MAKE IT MORE PLIABLE. ANY TEARS THAT OCCUR DURING THE PROCESS CAN BE MENDED ON THE BACK WITH TAPE AFTER THE PAPER HAS DRIED.

4. AFTER DRYING, FOLD THE BAG LENGTHWISE INTO THREE SECTIONS. FOLD IT IN HALF WIDTHWISE. THEN FOLD IT IN THIRDS. UNFOLD.

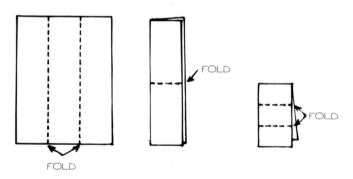

5. USING CRAYONS, DRAW SHORT HORIZONTAL LINES OR BLOCKS OF COLOR ABOUT 1 ½" LONG, DOWN THE VERTICAL LENGTH OF THE CLOTH. DRAW CRAYON LINES CLOSE TOGETHER, ALTERNATING BRIGHT COLORS AGAINST THE VERTICAL FOLDS.

6. WITH A BLACK FELT-TIPPED MARKER AND RULER, DRAW A FEW LINES TO OUTLINE THE SQUARES MADE BY THE FOLDS.

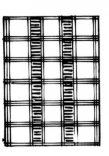

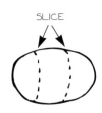

7. TO MAKE STAMPS, SLICE SMALL POTATOES INTO 1"–1 ½"-THICK SECTIONS.

8. WITH A PENCIL, OUTLINE A DESIGN ON THE POTATO SLICE. CREATE YOUR OWN DESIGNS AND SYMBOLS FOR STAMPS, OR USE THOSE PROVIDED IN THE ADINKRA DESIGNS AND SYMBOLS CHART ON PAGE 10.

9. CARVE OUT THE DESIGN WITH A KNIFE OR A SHARPENED TONGUE DEPRESSOR. USE CARE WHEN WORKING WITH ALL SHARP TOOLS, ESPECIALLY KNIVES.

10. PREPARE A STAMP PAD BY PLACING A SMALL, DAMP SPONGE IN A DISH. POUR ABOUT TWO TABLESPOONS OF BLACK TEMPERA PAINT ON THE SPONGE AND ALLOW THE PAINT TO SOAK INTO THE SPONGE.

11. PLAN THE ARRANGEMENT OF YOUR DESIGNS ON THE FABRIC. THEN, PRESS THE CARVED END OF THE POTATO AGAINST THE SPONGE, COATING IT WITH COLOR, AND STAMP IN THE APPROPRIATE SPOT. REPEAT THE PROCESS UNTIL ALL AREAS ARE PRINTED. ALLOW IT TO DRY.

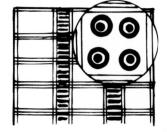

ADINKRA DESIGNS AND SYMBOLS

STAR

MOON AND STARS

HEART

FENCE

TEETH AND TONGUE

LADDER OF DEATH

HOURGLASS DRUM

GOD'S TREE

KING

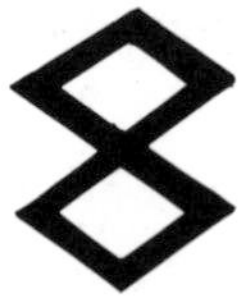

HANDCUFFS

FERN

SEEDS OF A PLANT

RAM'S HEAD

WOODEN COMB

BARK CLOTH

Bark cloth is made and used in several parts of the world. In Hawaii, it is known as tapa cloth and painted with bold geometric designs in earth colors, such as black, brown and white. In Mexico, the bark cloth is painted in bright colors depicting flora and fauna. In Africa, bark cloth was once used to make wearable garments. It has since been replaced by more durable clothing fabrics but continues to be made for ornamental purposes.

Today, bark cloth is most frequently found in Ghana and Nigeria. It is made from the inner bark of the Badie tree. When stripped, soaked and beaten, it produces a fine, soft material. In Uganda, the cloth is made from the bark of the fig tree. These fibers crisscross at right angles, like the threads of woven fabrics. After drying, most bark cloth is a light brown color. Since it is not woven, designs are stamped or painted on the surface.

THE BEST BARK CLOTH IS DECORATED WITH BLACK DYE AND MADE ESPECIALLY FOR ROYAL FAMILIES.

THE MBUTI PEOPLE LIVE IN THE ITURI FOREST, IN THE NORTHEAST CORNER OF ZAIRE. THEY ARE REFERRED TO AS A VANISHING PEOPLE.

BARK CLOTH DESIGN BY MBUTI PYGMIES.

BROWN BAG IDEA

MATERIALS and TOOLS

LARGE, PLAIN BROWN PAPER BAG

BLACK FELT-TIPPED MARKER OR CRAYON

PENCIL

RULER

SCISSORS

SINK OR LARGE BOWL OF WATER

DIRECTIONS

1. PREPARE THE PAPER BAG TO SIMULATE BARK CLOTH BY SOAKING IT IN WATER FOR ABOUT TEN MINUTES. THIS LOOSENS THE GLUED SEAMS.

2. OPEN THE BAG AND CAREFULLY SQUEEZE OUT THE EXCESS WATER.

3. GENTLY SPREAD OUT THE BAG ON NEWSPAPER TO DRY. SOAKING AND CRUSHING THE PAPER, THEN SQUEEZING OUT THE WATER, WILL MAKE IT MORE PLIABLE. ANY TEARS THAT OCCUR DURING THE PROCESS CAN BE MENDED ON THE BACK WITH TAPE AFTER THE PAPER HAS DRIED.

4. AFTER DRYING, DETERMINE THE SIZE OF YOUR PROJECT. A 12" × 18" PIECE IS A GOOD WORKING SIZE. CUT THIS PIECE FROM THE PREPARED PAPER.

5. SKETCH A DESIGN LIGHTLY ON THE PAPER. CONSIDER USING A VARIETY OF SIMPLE GEOMETRIC DESIGNS, SUCH AS TRIANGLES AND LINES, VARYING THEM IN BOTH RANDOM AND MORE FORMAL PATTERNS. USE A RULER FOR GEOMETRIC PATTERNS.

6. WITH A BLACK FELT-TIPPED MARKER OR CRAYON, CAREFULLY OUTLINE THE DESIGN.

7. ADD COLOR IN AREAS USING EARTH TONES, SUCH AS BLACK, GRAY, WHITE AND BRICK RED. USE CRAYONS, MARKERS OR TEMPERA PAINT.

BARK PAINTING DESIGNS

FANS

FANS ARE USED CEREMONIALLY AND FOR COOLING THROUGHOUT THE WORLD. THEY ARE OFTEN ASSOCIATED WITH CHINA AND JAPAN, WHERE THEY HAVE BEEN POPULAR SINCE ANCIENT TIMES. LIKE THE UMBRELLA AND THE FLY WHISK, THE FAN IS ALSO REGARDED AS A SYMBOL OF STATE IN MANY COUNTRIES OF THE EAST, EUROPE AND AFRICA.

FANS ARE A PART OF TRADITIONAL AFRICAN CEREMONIAL REGALIA. LARGE, CARVED, DECORATED FANS ARE CARRIED AND WAVED BY CHIEFS TO KEEP THE OBAS (RULER KINGS) COOL AS THEY HOLD COURT AND RECEIVE THEIR SUBJECTS.

FANS ARE MADE OF MANY DIFFERENT MATERIALS: IVORY, LEATHER, WOOD, VEGETABLE FIBER SUCH AS BARK AND PALM, AND TEXTILES SUCH AS COTTON, SILK AND VELVET. IN AFRICA, ANIMAL SKINS ARE USED MOST FREQUENTLY. LEATHERS FROM SMALL ANIMALS (GOATS AND SHEEP) ARE CALLED SKINS; THOSE

FROM LARGE ANIMALS (CAMELS AND CATTLE) ARE CALLED HIDES. PARCHMENT IS MADE FROM SPLIT SHEEPSKIN.

IN BENIN, NIGERIA, FANS ARE DECORATED WITH LEATHER LACING AND EMBROIDERY. HAIR IS LEFT INTACT ON THE BACKGROUND LEATHER. THE YORUBA OF NIGERIA DECORATE THEIR FANS WITH BEADS AND FEATHERS. COLORS ARE USUALLY RED, BLACK, BEIGE AND GREEN.

AFRICAN FANS CAN BE DIVIDED INTO THREE GROUPS: THE SCREEN, OR RIGID FAN; THE CEREMONIAL FAN; AND THE FOLDING FAN. THE RIGID FAN IS MADE OF MATERIAL STRETCHED OVER A ROUND OR OVAL FRAME. THE CEREMONIAL FAN IS OF LARGER PROPORTIONS THAN THE SCREEN FAN AND IS MOUNTED ON A LONG HANDLE. IT IS TRADITIONALLY USED IN ROYAL PROCESSIONS. THE FOLDING FAN IS COMPOSED OF A SEMI-CIRCULAR PIECE OF MATERIAL PRESSED INTO FOLDS, WITH STICKS INSERTED BETWEEN THE FOLDS FOR SUPPORT.

BROWN BAG IDEA

MATERIALS AND TOOLS

LARGE, PLAIN BROWN PAPER BAG

HEAVY YARN

THREAD

RULER

SCISSORS

WHITE GLUE

TWO STICKS (AS STRAIGHT AS POSSIBLE), SUCH AS DOWEL RODS, POTTED PLANT SUPPORT STICKS OR SECTIONS FROM OLD BAMBOO PLACEMATS OR SCREENS

NEEDLE

PENCIL

CRAYONS OR COLORED FELT-TIPPED MARKERS

DIRECTIONS

1. CUT THE PAPER BAG APART AT THE BACK SEAM, AND CUT OFF THE BOTTOM SECTION. SAVE THIS BOTTOM PIECE.

2. FOLD THE BAG IN HALF LENGTHWISE AND CUT ON THE FOLD.

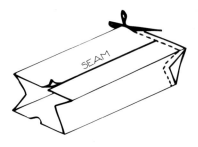

SEAM

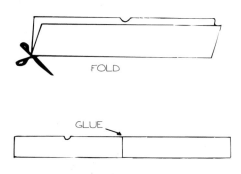

FOLD

GLUE

3. GLUE THE TWO SECTIONS TOGETHER, END-TO-END, FORMING ONE LONG STRIP. (LARGE BROWN PAPER BAGS MEASURE APPROX- IMATELY 36" WIDE WHEN OPENED FLAT. CUT IN HALF LENGTHWISE, YOU WILL HAVE ABOUT 72" OF PAPER FOR YOUR FAN.)

4. USE A PENCIL TO SKETCH YOUR DESIGN ON THE BAG, KEEPING IN MIND HOW THE FOLDS WILL EFFECT IT. LARGE, BOLD DESIGNS WORK BEST. USE CRAYONS OR FELT-TIPPED MARKERS TO COMPLETE THE DESIGN.

5. FOLD THE BAG ACCORDION-FASHION INTO EQUAL SECTIONS ABOUT 2 ¼" WIDE. FOR STRAIGHTER FOLDS, FIRST MAKE GUIDELINE FOLDS BY FOLDING YOUR STRIP IN HALF, CREASING THE FOLD WELL. NOW FOLD IN HALF AGAIN AND AGAIN AND AGAIN, IN PARALLEL FOLDS, UNTIL THE FOLDED STRIP IS AROUND 2" WIDE.

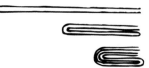

FOLD IN HALF,

IN HALF AGAIN,

IN HALF AGAIN (KEEP GOING).

REOPEN THE STRIP AND USE THE GUIDELINE FOLDS TO SHARPLY REFOLD THE STRIP IN ACCORDION FASHION.

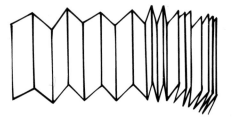

6. GLUE ONE STICK ON EITHER END OF THE ACCORDION FOLDS TO FORM THE FAN HANDLES.

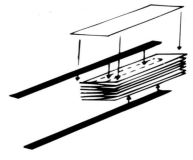

7. FROM THE RESERVED BOTTOM PART OF THE BAG, CUT TWO STRIPS THE SIZE OF THE END FAN FOLDS. GLUE THE STRIPS ON TOP OF THE END STICKS.

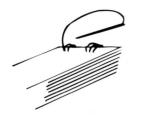

8. WITH THE NEEDLE AND DOUBLE THREAD, STITCH THROUGH THE TOP CORNERS OF THE FAN AND TIE. (DO NOT TIE THE THREAD TOO TIGHTLY.)

9. CUT A PIECE OF YARN APPROXIMATELY 12" LONG. GLUE THE CENTER OF YARN TO ONE SIDE OF THE FAN END PAPER, ABOUT 2" FROM THE PAPER'S BOTTOM. ALLOW THE GLUE TO DRY, THEN TURN THE FAN OVER AND TIE THE YARN ENDS TOGETHER TO KEEP THE FAN CLOSED.

GLUE

10. TO USE THE FAN, UNTIE AND OPEN AS SHOWN.

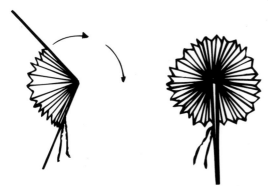

AFRICAN FAN DESIGNS

TRIBAL BEADS

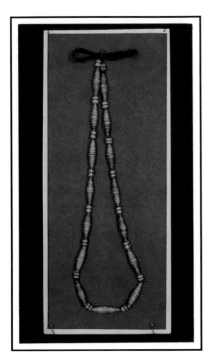

IN THE FOLKLORE OF EVERY LAND, BEADS HAVE BEEN ASSOCIATED WITH SOME PART OF THE CULTURE. THEY HAVE BEEN WORN AS ITEMS OF ADORNMENT FOR CENTURIES. MADE FROM AN INFINITE VARIETY OF MATERIALS, BEADS HAVE BEEN GIVEN SUCH NAMES AS FIDGET BEADS, WORRY BEADS, PRAYER BEADS, TRADE BEADS, BEGGAR BEADS AND NEED BEADS.

IN PREHISTORIC TIMES, BEADS WERE MADE OF BONE, TEETH, SHELLS, WOOD AND CLAY. THE EARLIEST MANUFACTURED GLASS BEADS CAME IN THE LATE FIFTEENTH CENTURY FROM EGYPT. CENTURIES BEFORE, BEADS OF GOLD AND PRECIOUS STONES WERE MADE IN CRETE. THEY HAVE ALSO BEEN MADE FROM CORAL, PEARLS, AMBER, SILVER, COPPER, BRASS, NUTS, FEATHERS, LEATHER, CLAWS, OSTRICH EGGS, BAMBOO, SEEDS AND PLASTIC. AFRICAN GLASS BEADS ARE MADE FROM CRUSHED BOTTLES. A PIECE OF STRAW PLACED IN THE CENTER OF EACH BEAD CREATES THE HOLE FOR STRINGING. THE STRAW BURNS AWAY DURING THE FIRING OF THE BEADS.

In africa, beads and shells adorn musical instruments, calabashes (gourds) and royal headdresses. The cowrie shell was used as a medium of exchange and, as such, greatly increased the value of items they adorned. Today, they are still one of the most common adornments for masks and headdresses. Amber and carnelian beads also have great value as symbols of prestige and wealth. They are worn to indicate royalty and authority by chieftains. Women wear them to emphasize their beauty. The hausa tribe and the women of mali are known for the fine crafting of their beads and their high-quality beadwork.

Of the european beads brought to africa for trade, the millefiores were among the most prized. They are brilliantly colored with an intricate pattern. First brought to africa in the sixteenth century, the millefiores (a thousand flowers) are a timeless example of technical and aesthetic achievement. They are made from long, brightly colored rods of molten glass that are cut into thin sections and arranged next to each other on a flat surface. A tube of hot glass is rolled over this delicately arranged pattern of colorful chips, sealing the chips to the tube and creating an oblong bead with a vibrant surface pattern.

MILLEFIORES BEADS

The chevron, a highly desirable trade bead produced in amsterdam, is white glass layered with blue, with a starburst pattern visible on the end. Snake bone beads are another striking example from europe. They are colorful zigzag beads that fit together like vertebrae in a string of alternating colors.

BROWN BAG IDEA

MATERIALS and TOOLS

    LARGE, PLAIN BROWN PAPER BAG

    GLUE

    FELT-TIPPED MARKERS

    STRING OR YARN

    ROUND TOOTHPICKS

    SCISSORS

    RULER

    PENCIL

DIRECTIONS

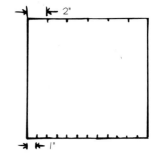

1. CUT A PIECE APPROXIMATELY 12"
    SQUARE FROM A BROWN PAPER BAG.

2. START AT THE TOP LEFT-HAND
    CORNER OF THE SQUARE AND MARK
    OFF 2" SECTIONS.

3. START AT THE BOTTOM LEFT-HAND
    CORNER OF THE SQUARE AND MARK
    OFF 1" SECTIONS.

4. USE A PENCIL TO DRAW A LINE FROM THE TOP LEFT-HAND
    CORNER OF THE SQUARE TO THE MARK 1" IN FROM THE
    BOTTOM LEFT-HAND CORNER.

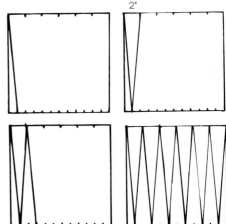

5. DRAW A LINE FROM THE
    1" MARK UP TO THE TOP 2"
    MARK.

6. DRAW A LINE FROM THE
    2" MARK ON THE TOP OF
    THE PAPER TO THE 3"
    MARK ON THE BOTTOM
    OF THE PAPER.

7. REPEAT UNTIL YOU
    REACH THE RIGHT-HAND
    SIDE OF THE PAPER,
    CREATING A SERIES OF
    TRIANGLES.

8. CUT OUT THE TRIANGLES.

9. ROLL THE WIDE END OF A TRIANGLE AROUND A TOOTHPICK.

10. CONTINUE ROLLING UNTIL YOU REACH THE POINT OF THE TRIANGLE. PUT A BIT OF GLUE ON THE POINT AND SEAL IT TO THE BEAD.

11. PULL THE TOOTHPICK OUT AND REPEAT THE PROCESS FOR THE REST OF THE BEADS.

12. THREAD THE BEADS ON A PIECE OF STRING OR YARN AND TIE FOR A NECKLACE.

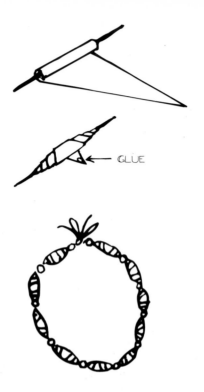

NOTE

• VARY THE WIDTH AND LENGTH OF THE PAPER TRIANGLES TO MAKE LONG AND FAT BEADS.

 • STRAIGHT STRIPS OF PAPER MAKE CYLINDRICAL BEADS.

 • CYLINDRICAL BEADS CAN BE ROLLED ONE AROUND THE OTHER TO MAKE COMPLEX SHAPES.

• FOR A LINE PATTERN ON THE BEAD, DRAW THE LINES MARKING OFF THE TRIANGLES WITH A ¼" WIDE FELT-TIPPED PEN, AND CUT IN THE MIDDLE OF THOSE LINES.

• MAGAZINE PAGES MAKE ATTRACTIVE PAPER BEADS.

• FOR VARIETY, ADD A FEW GLASS OR WOOD BEADS TO YOUR PAPER BEAD NECKLACE.

LEATHER SHIELDS

NIMAL SKINS HAVE ALWAYS BEEN IMPORTANT TO PEOPLE AS A SOURCE OF CLOTHING, SHELTER, AND PROTECTION FROM ENEMIES. TRADITIONALLY, THE QUANTITY AND QUALITY OF THE SKINS POSSESSED DESIGNATED A PERSON'S WEALTH. IN AFRICA, LEATHER STILL PLAYS AN IMPORTANT ROLE IN THE DAILY LIVES OF ITS PEOPLE. BAGS, WATERPROOF CONTAINERS, FANS, GARMENTS, JEWELRY, TENTS, HASSOCKS AND SADDLES ARE MADE BY NATIVE CRAFTSPEOPLE AND DECORATED IN STYLES PARTICULAR TO EACH GEOGRAPHIC AREA.

THE PROCESS OF TANNING TO ARREST DECOMPOSITION DATES BACK TO THE BRONZE AGE. PREPARATION OF SKINS AND HIDES REQUIRES SCRAPING AWAY THE FATTY LAYERS UNDER THE SKIN, CUTTING AWAY THE HAIR, WASHING AND TANNING, THEN TREATING WITH A FINAL DRESSING TO MAKE THE MATERIAL MORE PLIABLE. LEATHER FROM A SMALL ANIMAL IS CALLED A SKIN; FROM A LARGE ANIMAL, THE LEATHER IS CALLED A HIDE.

CATTLE, GOAT, SHEEP, CAMEL AND OXEN HIDES ARE THE MOST POPULAR.

ORNATE AFRICAN LEATHER SHIELDS ARE MADE IN A GREAT VARIETY OF SIZES, SHAPES AND COLORS. THEY ARE EMBELLISHED WITH FUR, BEADS, SHELLS, SEEDS, BRASS ORNAMENTS AND FEATHERS. SHAPES OF SHIELDS VARY WITH EACH TRIBE. SHIELDS FROM KENYA ARE ROUND WITH PAINTED DESIGNS. THE ZULUS MAKE NARROW, OVAL SHIELDS. THE MASAI BUFFALO HIDE SHIELDS ARE PARTICULARLY TOUGH AND HARD, MAKING PENETRATION DIFFICULT. MASAI DESIGNS ARE PAINTED IN EARTH TONES, WITH PIGMENTS MADE FROM OCHRE, CHARCOAL AND RED EARTH. EACH WARRIOR PAINTS HIS OWN SHIELD, RECORDING HIS DEEDS OF BRAVERY.

BROWN BAG IDEA

MATERIALS AND TOOLS

LARGE, PLAIN BROWN PAPER BAG

BROWN TEMPERA PAINT

LIGHTWEIGHT CARDBOARD (NOT CORRUGATED)

PENCIL

YARN

GLUE

FELT-TIPPED MARKERS OR CRAYONS

SCISSORS

LARGE NAIL (FOR PUNCHING HOLES)

SINK OR LARGE BOWL OF WATER

DIRECTIONS

1. FILL YOUR SINK OR BOWL ½ FULL WITH WARM WATER. ADD ½ CUP OF BROWN WATERBASED TEMPERA PAINT. CRUMPLE THE BAG AND PLACE IT IN THE PAINT SOLUTION.

2. SOAK THE BAG IN THE TEMPERA SOLUTION FOR ABOUT TEN MINUTES. THIS LOOSENS THE GLUED SEAMS. OPEN THE BAG AND CAREFULLY SQUEEZE OUT THE EXCESS WATER. GENTLY SPREAD OUT THE BAG ON NEWSPAPER TO DRY. ANY TEARS THAT OCCUR DURING THE PROCESS CAN BE MENDED ON THE BACK WITH TAPE AFTER THE PAPER HAS DRIED.

3. FOLD THE BAG IN HALF. DRAW ½ OF AN OVAL SHAPE CENTERED ON THE FOLDED EDGE.

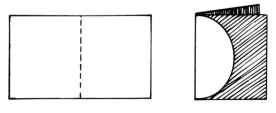

4. CUT OUT THE OVAL.

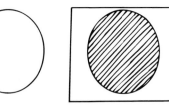

5. PLACE THE PAPER OVAL ON A PIECE OF LIGHT-WEIGHT CARDBOARD AND TRACE AROUND IT WITH A PENCIL.

6. INSIDE THE TRACING, SKETCH ANOTHER OVAL ON THE CARDBOARD ONE INCH SMALLER ALL THE WAY AROUND. CUT OUT THE SMALLER, INNER CARDBOARD OVAL.

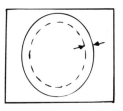

7. DECORATE YOUR PAPER SHIELD WITH CRAYONS OR FELT-TIPPED MARKERS, ALLOWING A 1" BORDER AROUND THE EDGE.

8. PLACE THE DECORATED PAPER FRONT-SIDE DOWN ON THE TABLE.

9. PUT GLUE ON ONE SIDE OF THE CARDBOARD OVAL.

10. PLACE THE GLUED CARDBOARD SURFACE ON THE BACK OF THE DECORATED PAPER, LEAVING AN EVEN BORDER OF 1" OR MORE AROUND THE CARDBOARD.

11. PUT GLUE ON THE BACK OF THE PAPER SHIELD'S EXPOSED EDGE AND FOLD IT OVER THE CARDBOARD OVAL.

12. CUT ANOTHER OVAL, ½" SMALLER THAN THE DECORATED SHIELD, FROM ANOTHER PLAIN, BROWN PAPER BAG AND GLUE IT OVER THE BACK OF THE CARDBOARD SHIELD. (OPTIONAL.)

13. PUNCH FOUR HOLES (TWO POSITIONED STRAIGHT ACROSS FROM THE OTHER TWO), 1" FROM THE EDGE OF THE SHIELD.

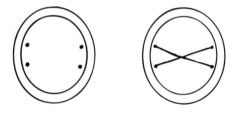

14. THREAD A PIECE OF YARN OR CORD THROUGH THE HOLES SO THAT IT TIES ON THE BACKSIDE OF THE SHIELD.

15. THE CORD ON THE FRONT SIDE OF THE SHIELD SHOULD LOOK LIKE THE DRAWING.

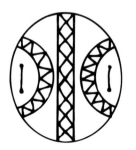

DASHIKIS

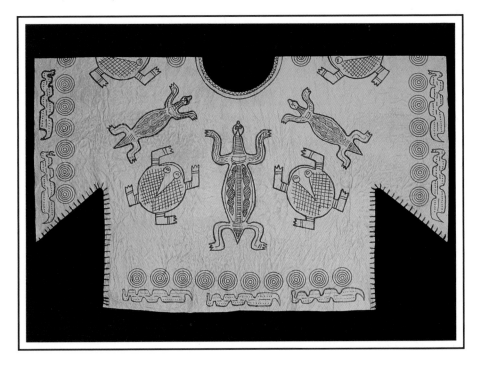

THE DASHIKI ORIGINATED AS A SHIRT WORN BY THE MEN OF WEST AFRICA. IT IS SIMPLE IN DESIGN AND COMFORTABLE TO WEAR. SOME DASHIKIS ARE WORN SHORT, AND OTHERS ARE WORN BELOW THE KNEES. IN THE UNITED STATES, THE DASHIKI IS WORN BY BOTH MEN AND WOMEN.

DASHIKIS ARE MADE FROM ONE PIECE OF FABRIC AND REQUIRE ONLY TWO SEAMS. BATIK AND EMBROIDERY TECHNIQUES ARE USED FOR DECORATION. IN WEST AFRICAN CITIES, IT IS POSSIBLE TO SELECT A PIECE OF FABRIC AND HAVE A DASHIKI MADE BY A SIDEWALK TAILOR WHILE YOU WAIT.

BROWN BAG IDEA

MATERIALS AND TOOLS

TWO LARGE, PLAIN BROWN PAPER BAGS

YARN

FELT-TIPPED PENS OR CRAYONS

SCISSORS

LARGE NEEDLE

SINK OR LARGE BOWL OF WATER

DIRECTIONS

1. PREPARE THE PAPER BAGS TO SIMULATE CLOTH BY SOAKING THEM IN WATER FOR ABOUT TEN MINUTES. THIS LOOSENS THE GLUED SEAMS.

2. OPEN THE BAGS AND CAREFULLY SQUEEZE OUT THE EXCESS WATER.

3. GENTLY SPREAD OUT THE BAGS ON NEWSPAPER TO DRY. SOAKING AND CRUSHING THE PAPER, THEN SQUEEZING OUT THE WATER, WILL MAKE IT MORE PLIABLE. ANY TEARS THAT OCCUR DURING THE PROCESS CAN BE MENDED ON THE BACK WITH TAPE AFTER THE PAPER HAS DRIED.

4. PRESS THE PAPER WITH A WARM IRON. WHEN IRONING, BE CAREFUL NOT TO LET THE PAPER GET TOO HOT, AS THIS MAY CAUSE IT TO BURN. BE SURE TO USE APPROPRIATE SAFETY PRECAUTIONS WHEN WORKING WITH IRONS AND OTHER ELECTRICAL APPLIANCES. PROPER SAFETY MEASURES WILL HELP PREVENT FIRE AND INJURY.

5. GLUE THE TWO BAGS TOGETHER, LEAVING A 1"–2" WIDE OVERLAPPED SEAM. ALLOW THE GLUE TO DRY.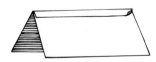

6. FOLD THE GLUED BAGS INTO FOURTHS.

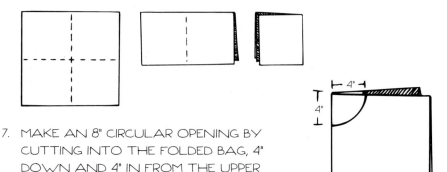

7. MAKE AN 8" CIRCULAR OPENING BY CUTTING INTO THE FOLDED BAG, 4" DOWN AND 4" IN FROM THE UPPER LEFT CORNER.

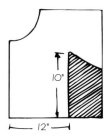

8. ON THE PAPER'S BOTTOM EDGE, MEASURE IN 12" FROM THE LEFT SIDE AND UP 10" FROM THE BOTTOM. CUT AWAY THE AREA SHOWN AS SHADED IN THE ILLUSTRATION TO FASHION THE SLEEVES.

9. OPEN THE FOLDED PAPER AND SEW UP THE SIDES AND UNDER THE ARMS USING THE YARN AND NEEDLE.

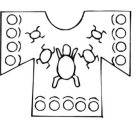

10. DECORATE THE DASHIKI WITH CRAYONS OR FELT-TIPPED MARKERS. THE DESIGNS MAY BE GEOMETRIC OR FIGURATIVE. LARGE, BOLD SYMBOLS WORK WELL IN COMBINATION WITH SMALL, REPEATED PATTERNS.

AFRICAN DESIGNS

ETHIOPIAN MAGIC SCROLLS

ETHIOPIA IS A MULTIRACIAL NATION. ALTHOUGH MANY LANGUAGES ARE SPOKEN, IT IS THROUGH THE LANGUAGE OF THE VISUAL ARTS THAT THIS COMPLEX EMPIRE IS REVEALED. THE DESIGN MOTIFS OF ETHIOPIA REFLECT THREE OF THE WORLD'S GREAT RELIGIONS, WHICH PERMEATE AND COEXIST IN THE CULTURE: JUDAISM, CHRISTIANITY AND ISLAM. THE BEAUTY OF THE COUNTRY'S RELIGIOUS ARTIFACTS, SUCH AS ILLUMINATED MANUSCRIPTS AND ICONS ON WOOD, HAS HAD LITTLE EXPOSURE TO THE MAINSTREAM OF HISTORY. CREATED FOR DEVOTIONAL USE, THESE CULTURAL TREASURES HAVE BEEN PRESERVED FOR CENTURIES IN THE CHAMBERS OF ETHIOPIAN HOUSES OF WORSHIP.

ETHIOPIAN MAGIC SCROLLS WERE MADE OF LONG, NARROW BANDS OF PARCHMENT ON WHICH THE IMAGES OF CHRISTIAN SAINTS ALTERNATED WITH DEMON-LIKE MASKS, ALL INTERLACED WITH PATTERNS, ROSETTES AND STYLIZED CROSSES. THE SIGNS AND SYMBOLS FOUND ON THE SCROLLS

EXHIBIT A DISTINCTIVE USE AND COMBINATION OF LINE, FORM AND COLOR. THE SCROLLS WERE PREPARED BY PRIESTS, CALLED "DABTARAS," AND WERE INTENDED AS TALISMANS OR CHARMS TO PROTECT THE WEARER.

THE SCROLLS WERE MADE OF PARCHMENT PREPARED FROM SHEEPSKIN. THE PARCHMENT WAS CUT INTO THREE STRIPS OF EQUAL WIDTH AND SEWN TOGETHER END-TO-END SO THAT THE FINAL LENGTH OF THE SCROLL EQUALS THE HEIGHT OF THE BENEFICIARY, PROTECTING THE PERSON FROM HEAD TO FOOT. THE DABTARA PREPARES THE COLORS FOR THE INKS TO BE USED. SOOT SCRAPED FROM THE BOT.TOM OF POTS IS USED TO MAKE BLACK; ROOTS, FLOWER AND FRUIT JUICES PRODUCE RED; FLOWER PETALS AND EGG YOLKS MAKE YELLOW; AND GREEN LEAVES RENDER GREEN. THE SCROLLS WERE ENCASED IN LEATHER AND HUNG FROM AROUND THE WEARER'S NECK BY A LEATHER STRAP.

THERE WERE TWO TYPES OF PAINTING ON THE SCROLLS: FIGURATIVE AND NON-FIGURATIVE, OR TALISMANS. THE FIGURATIVE PAINTINGS TOLD THE STORY OF A PERSON AND REPRESENTED THE REAL APPEARANCE OF THINGS, AS IN A PHOTOGRAPH. THE TALISMAN HAD A GEOMETRIC STYLE AND REPRESENTED WHAT IS HIDDEN OR INVISIBLE, SUCH AS A SPIRIT. THE INDIVIDUAL PAINTINGS ON THE SCROLLS MEASURE ABOUT TWO INCHES SQUARE. DESIGNS FEATURING EYES WERE TYPICAL OF TALISMAN SCROLL ART. THE PURPOSE OF THESE DESIGNS WAS TO REINFORCE THE POWER OF THE EYES FOR THE PROTECTION OF THE PERSON FOR WHOM THEY WERE MADE. EYES POINTING IN ALL DIRECTIONS SIGNIFIED THE CLIENT WAS PROTECTED IN ALL DIRECTIONS. FACES WERE ALMOST ALWAYS PAINTED IN RED.

SYMBOLS WORN AS TALISMANS OR CHARMS ARE WELL KNOWN TO US TODAY. AMONG SUCH SYMBOLS ARE THE HEX SIGN PAINTED ON BARNS THROUGHOUT PENNSYLVANIA FOR PROTECTION AGAINST FIRE AND LIGHTENING, AND THE EGG AS A TOKEN OF LOVE, OFTEN EXCHANGED AT EASTER. ANOTHER SYMBOL IS THE POMANDER MADE FROM AN ORANGE, CONSIDERED A FRUIT OF LOVE AND FERTILITY, PIERCED WITH CLOVES TO REPRESENT THE PRESERVATION OF LOVE.

BROWN BAG IDEA

MATERIALS AND TOOLS

LARGE, PLAIN BROWN PAPER BAG

RULER

PENCIL

PLAIN OR GRAPH PAPER

SCISSORS

FELT-TIPPED MARKERS

GLUE

DIRECTIONS

1. MAKE A LIST OF SYMBOLS THAT MIGHT BE USED TO REPRESENT EACH OF THE FOLLOWING:

   PEACE (DOVE)   HALLOWEEN (PUMPKIN)

   LOVE (HEART)   STUBBORNNESS (DONKEY)

   WISDOM (OWL)   BIRTHDAY (CAKE)

   OLYMPICS (TORCH)   GOOD LUCK (FOUR-LEAF CLOVER)

   SLY (FOX)   COURAGE (LION)

2. CHOOSE A SYMBOL THAT HAS SPECIAL MEANING FOR YOU OR USE ONE FROM THE PRECEDING LIST. USE GRAPH PAPER OR MAKE YOUR OWN GRID ON PLAIN PAPER WITH A RULER AND PENCIL.

   START WITH THREE SQUARE SHAPES. IN THE FIRST SQUARE, DRAW A REALISTIC REPRESENTATION OF YOUR SYMBOL. IN THE SECOND SQUARE, DESIGN A SIMPLIFIED, GEOMETRIC ABSTRACTION OF THE SYMBOL. IN THE THIRD SQUARE, CREATE A DECORATIVE TALISMAN OF YOUR SYMBOL BY FURTHER SIMPLIFYING THE DESIGN AND REPEATING THE MOTIF WITHIN THE SQUARE. YOU CAN INCREASE OR REDUCE THE SIZE OF THE ORIGINAL ABSTRACTED DESIGN AND/OR BLOCK OUT SOLID AREAS OF COLOR WITHIN THE DESIGN. SEE HOW MANY WAYS YOU CAN DESIGN YOUR SYMBOL INTO A PATTERN. YOU WILL BE EVOLVING AN ORIGINAL DESIGN FROM A NATURAL OBJECT OR OBJECTS. LET THE SHAPE SUGGEST THE MOST SIMPLE GEOMETRIC FORM OF THE OBJECT. TRY REPEATING THIS GEOMETRIC DESIGN TO CREATE A PATTERN. CREATE OTHER MOTIFS USING DIFFERENT

COMBINATIONS AND DIVISIONS OF THE ORIGINAL FORM AND SHAPE.

3. CUT THREE 10" OR 12" SQUARE SECTIONS OF PAPER FROM THE BROWN PAPER BAG, WHICH WILL REPRESENT THE PARCHMENT BACKGROUND.

4. GLUE THE STRIPS TOGETHER END-TO-END TO CREATE A SINGLE LONG SCROLL.

5. DECIDE THE NUMBER OF SPACES AND REPETITIONS OF YOUR DESIGN YOU WOULD LIKE. DESIGNS MAY BE REPEATED SEVERAL TIMES IN DIFFERENT DIRECTIONS. LIMIT YOURSELF TO THREE COLORS AND BLACK.

GOOD LUCK

THE EYE AS A DESIGN MOTIF

REALISTIC   ABSTRACTION   DECORATIVE (TALISMAN)

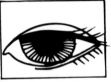
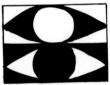

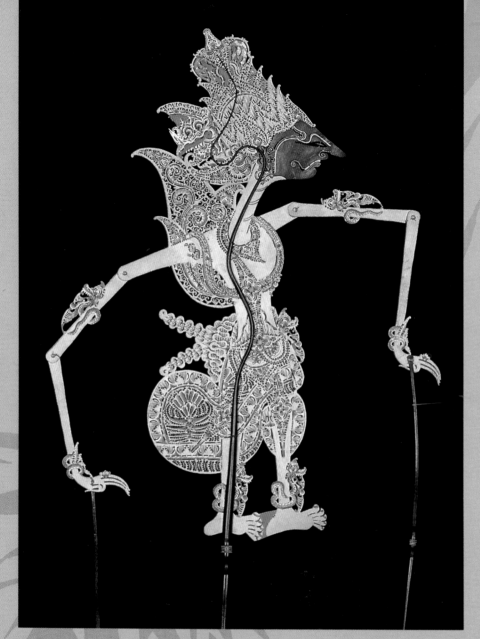

SHADOW PUPPET FROM JAVA.

ASIA AND THE MIDDLE EAST

INDIAN SHISHA MIRROR VESTS   36

JAVANESE SHADOW PUPPETS   40

JAPANESE DECORATIVE PAPER   47

ISRAELI MARBLE MOSAICS   52

INDIAN SHISHA MIRROR VESTS

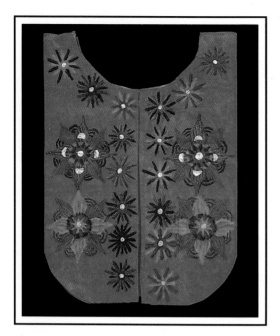

Shishadur, or mirror embroidery, is the ancient East Indian art of stitching bits of mica or mirror to cloth. It is used for decorating clothing as well as wall hangings, rugs and personal accessories. Each region within East India produces embroidered items with patterns that are unique to that area.

Locally available natural dyes account for the traditional colorings of fabrics and threads. Some of the most common dyes are madder root and the cochineal insect (reds), indigo (blues or purples), saffron (yellow) and iron filings (black). Both the design and coloring of embroidery are connected with Hindu religious beliefs. Red and yellow, colors of joy, are often used.

The minute pieces of silvered glass or mica are attached to the ground fabric by a network of

STITCHERY AROUND THEIR EDGES. THESE WEBS ARE FURTHER SECURED WITH THE BLANKET OR BUTTONHOLE BINDING STITCH. SHISHA STITCH, NAMED FOR THIS TYPE OF EMBROIDERY, IS A DESCRIPTIVE NAME FOR ANY OF THE STITCHES USED FOR SEWING DOWN SHISHA GLASS.

BROWN BAG IDEA

MATERIALS AND TOOLS

LARGE, PLAIN BROWN PAPER BAG

RED TEMPERA PAINT

LARGE PAINT BRUSH

ALUMINUM FOIL (SMALL MIRRORS ARE READILY AVAILABLE FROM CRAFT SUPPLIERS. PIECES OF MYLAR OR SILVER PLASTIC MAY ALSO BE USED. FOR THE MIRRORS IN OUR SHISHA VESTS, WE WILL USE ALUMINUM FOIL.)

TAPE

CRAYONS OR FELT-TIPPED MARKERS

SCISSORS

RULER

PAPER PUNCH (OPTIONAL.)

SMALL BOWL

SINK OR LARGE BOWL OF WATER.

DIRECTIONS

1. GIVE THE PAPER BAG A CLOTH-LIKE TEXTURE BY SOAKING IT IN WATER FOR ABOUT TEN MINUTES.

2. CAREFULLY SQUEEZE OUT THE EXCESS WATER, AND GENTLY LAY THE BAG OUT ON A NEWSPAPER-COVERED TABLE.

3. DILUTE THE PAINT IN A SMALL BOWL, APPROXIMATELY TWO PARTS WATER TO ONE PART PAINT.

4. WHILE THE BAG IS STILL DAMP, PAINT ITS ENTIRE OUTSIDE SURFACE WITH THE DILUTED PAINT MIXTURE.

5. WHILE IT IS STILL WET, CRUSH THE BAG CAREFULLY. THIS WILL HELP THE PAINT PENETRATE THE PAPER, SIMULATING DYED FABRIC.

6. FLATTEN THE BAG GENTLY TO ITS ORIGINAL SHAPE AND ALLOW IT TO DRY. ANY TEARS THAT OCCUR DURING THE PROCESS CAN BE MENDED ON THE INSIDE WITH TAPE AFTER THE BAG HAS DRIED.

7. MAKE A LENGTHWISE CENTER CREASE IN THE BOTTOM OF THE BAG BY FOLDING ONE EDGE TO MEET THE OTHER.

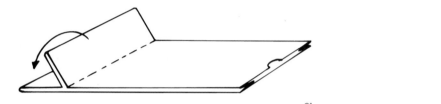

8. WITH THE BAG FLAT ON THE TABLE, MARK THE NECKLINE MEASUREMENTS (2"-WIDE SHOULDER STRAPS, 4"-DEEP FRONT AND BACK NECKLINES) AND BOTTOM EDGES (CORNERS ROUNDED TO 3" UP AND 3" IN FROM THE SIDES) AS SHOWN IN THE ILLUSTRATION. CUT ALONG THE MEASURED LINES.

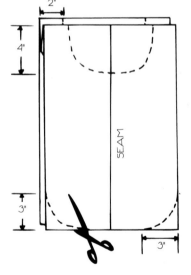

9. CUT THE VEST FRONT OPENING ALONG THE SEAM OF THE BAG. (THE STORE LOGO, IF THERE IS ONE, SHOULD BE ON THE BACK.)

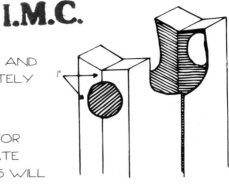

10. OPEN THE SIDES OF THE BAG AND CUT ARMHOLES APPROXIMATELY 1" FROM THE SIDE EDGES AND SHOULDERS.

11. LIGHTLY PENCIL IN DESIGNS FOR SHISHA EMBROIDERY. DESIGNATE AREAS WHERE SMALL HOLES WILL BE PUNCHED OR CUT FOR "MIRRORS." LIGHTLY PENCIL IN THE "EMBROIDERY" DESIGNS AROUND THEM.

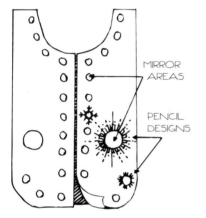

MIRROR AREAS

PENCIL DESIGNS

12. CUT OR PUNCH HOLES IN THE VEST, FRONT AND BACK, FOR THE "MIRRORS."

13. TAPE SMALL PIECES OF FOIL ON THE INSIDE OF THE VEST, COVERING THE HOLES. MAKE SURE THE SHINY SIDE SHOWS THROUGH THE HOLE.

14. PROCEED TO DECORATE AROUND THE "MIRRORS" WITH CRAYON OR FELT-TIPPED MARKER DESIGNS. EXAMPLES OF TYPICAL SHISHA DESIGNS ARE SHOWN IN THE ILLUSTRATION. TRY VARIATIONS OF YOUR OWN. DON'T FORGET TO DESIGN THE BACK OF THE VEST AS WELL!

NOTE: OTHER ARTICLES OF CLOTHING AND ACCESSORIES, SUCH AS BELTS OR PURSES, CAN BE MADE WITH BROWN BAGS AND THE SHISHA TECHNIQUE. ALSO, ANOTHER BACKGROUND COLOR, SUCH AS BLUE OR PURPLE, COULD BE USED FOR YOUR VEST.

JAVANESE SHADOW PUPPETS

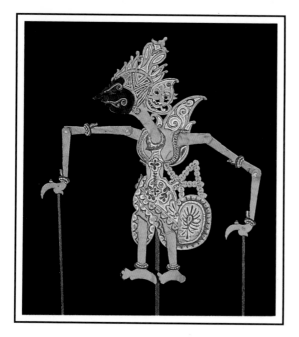

Through the centuries, Indonesia has developed a tradition of puppetry. The most elaborate presentations are found on Java, an island of Indonesia. There, puppetry encompasses religion plus many of the arts of the region: music, sculpture, painting and drama. Performances present stories of eternal conflict between good, always placed on the right of the stage, and evil, positioned on the left.

The term wayang applies to dance and theater as well as to puppetry. Wayang means shadow and is also the name used for the puppets that appear in the plays. There are three forms of Javanese puppets: the wayang kulit (a shadow puppet), the wayang klitik (a flat, wooden puppet) and the wayang golek (a wooden rod puppet).

The wayang kulit play is a dramatic, exciting performance popular among all Javanese social

CLASSES. KULIT MEANS LEATHER; THUS, WAYANG KULIT MEANS "SHADOWS OF PUPPETS MADE FROM LEATHER." THE PUPPETS ARE ACTUALLY MADE OF PARCHMENT, WHICH IS LEATHER THAT HAS BEEN SCRAPED THIN, POLISHED AND USED AS A MATERIAL TO WRITE OR PAINT ON.

THE WAYANG KULIT SHADOW PLAYS ARE BASED ON THE INDIAN EPICS OF THE RAMAYANA AND THE MAHABARATA, WHICH WERE TRANSLATED INTO JAVANESE. THE JAVANESE MODIFIED AND REINTERPRETED THE MATERIAL TO CREATE A RICH HINDU-JAVANESE VERSION. EACH PUPPET REPRESENTS A PERSON IN THE STORY. THE NUMBER OF PUPPETS MAY VARY FROM AS FEW AS SEVENTY TO SEVERAL HUNDRED.

WAYANG KULIT PUPPETS ARE NOT MEANT TO BE REPRESENTATIONAL BUT RATHER HIGHLY STYLIZED FIGURES GIVEN SHAPES THAT SYMBOLIZE CERTAIN TYPES OF CHARACTERS. GOOD CHARACTERS ARE ELEGANTLY REPRESENTED BY REFINED FEATURES, WITH HEADS SLOPING FORWARD ON BENT NECKS, THIN POINTED NOSES AND DELICATE, GRACEFUL BODIES. BAD CHARACTERS ARE LARGER, WITH BULGING EYES, BULBOUS NOSES, THICK LIPS AND ROTUND BODIES. THE COLOR OF THE FACE ALSO EXPRESSES THE NATURE OF THE PUPPET. WHITE AND GOLD REPRESENT YOUTH AND BEAUTY, THE GOOD QUALITIES OF A PERSON. BLACK SYMBOLIZES WISDOM AND TRANQUILITY, AND A RED FACE TYPIFIES CRUELTY, GREED, COWARDICE AND COARSENESS. COSTUME AND HEADDRESS STYLES ALSO HELP IDENTIFY CHARACTERS.

WAYANG KULIT PUPPETS' BODIES HAVE LONG ARMS THAT ARE JOINTED AT THE SHOULDERS AND ELBOWS. THE FIGURES ARE CONTROLLED BY THREE RODS MADE FROM BUFFALO HORNS. THE LARGEST ROD SUPPORTS THE BODY, AND THE OTHER TWO CONTROL THE ARMS, WHICH ARE ATTACHED TO THE BODY WITH STRING. PUPPETS RANGE IN SIZE FROM ONE TO THREE FEET TALL.

THESE PUPPETS ARE MADE FROM THE HIDE OF THE WATER BUFFALO. FIRST, THE HAIR IS REMOVED AND THE SKIN IS SCRAPED TO MAKE IT THIN AND TRANSLUCENT. NEXT, THE BODY AND ITS SEPARATE ARMS ARE CUT FROM THE HIDE. THE BODY IS THEN INCISED WITH AN ASSORTMENT OF CHISELS TO CREATE A SERIES

A SERIES OF HOLES AND OPENINGS IN THE SURFACE THAT WILL
RESULT IN INTERESTING SHADOW PATTERNS. THE PUPPET IS
THEN PAINTED. THE ARTIST'S BASIC PALETTE CONSISTS OF
GOLD, BLACK, WHITE AND THREE PRIMARY COLORS. THE PUPPET
IS PAINTED ON BOTH SIDES AND VARNISHED BEFORE SUPPORT
STICKS AND ARM RODS ARE ADDED.

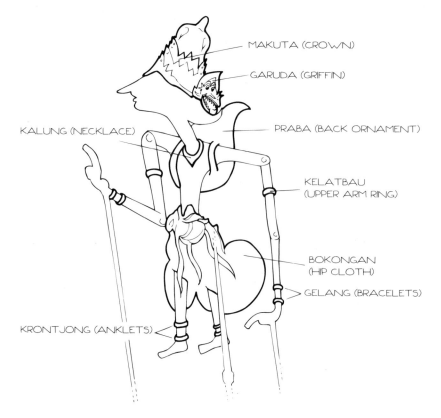

MAKUTA (CROWN)

GARUDA (GRIFFIN)

KALUNG (NECKLACE)

PRABA (BACK ORNAMENT)

KELATBAU
(UPPER ARM RING)

BOKONGAN
(HIP CLOTH)

GELANG (BRACELETS)

KRONTJONG (ANKLETS)

THE PERSON WHO BRINGS ALL THE IDEAS AND PUPPETS
TOGETHER IS CALLED THE DALANG. THE DALANG
MANIPULATES THE PUPPETS, RECITES OR SINGS THE TEXT, AND
CONDUCTS THE SMALL ORCHESTRA KNOWN AS THE GAMELAN,
WHICH ACCOMPANIES ALL PERFORMANCES. THE DALANG, OR
PUPPETEER, SITS BEHIND A LARGE SCREEN OF WHITE LINEN
APPROXIMATELY TEN FEET LONG BY FIVE FEET WIDE, WHICH IS
STRETCHED OVER A WOOD OR BAMBOO FRAME. A LARGE
COPPER LAMP IS POSITIONED OVERHEAD TO THROW PUPPET
SILHOUETTES ONTO THE SCREEN. THE DALANG CANNOT BE
SEEN FROM THE SHADOW SIDE OF THE SCREEN. ALONG THE
BOTTOM OF THE SCREEN FRAME IS A LONG TRUNK OF A
BANANA PALM. INTO THIS, THE DALANG STICKS THE HORN

HORN SUPPORTS FOR EACH PUPPET, ARRANGED IN THE ORDER OF HEIGHT, WITH THE TALLEST PLACED AT THE OUTER ENDS. THE GOOD CHARACTER PUPPETS ARE PLACED ON THE RIGHT SIDE OF THE SCREEN, AND THE CRUDE OR EVIL ONES ARE POSITIONED ON THE LEFT. THE SPACE IN THE MIDDLE IS RESERVED FOR A TREE-SHAPED WAYANG, CALLED A GUNUNGAN. THIS ELABORATELY INCISED AND DECORATED FAN-SHAPED PUPPET REPRESENTS THE SCENERY. IT CAN BE MOVED SO THAT IT SUGGESTS MOVING WATER, CLOUDS OR FLICKERING FLAMES. IT IS ALSO USED TO DESIGNATE THE BEGINNING AND END OF THE PLAY.

PERFORMANCES LAST FROM SHORTLY AFTER SUNDOWN UNTIL DAWN. PLAYS HAVE TWO AUDIENCES: THE WOMEN, WHO SEE ONLY THE SHADOWS PROJECTED ON THE SCREEN, AND THE MEN, WHO SIT ON THE SIDE OF THE DALANG AND CAN ENJOY THE COLORS OF THE FIGURES AND SEE THE DALANG MANIPULATE THE PUPPETS.

BROWN BAG IDEA

MATERIALS AND TOOLS

LARGE, PLAIN BROWN PAPER BAG

PLAIN DRAWING PAPER

SCISSORS

UTILITY KNIFE AND/OR PAPER PUNCHES OF DIFFERENT SIZES

THREE STRAIGHT STICKS, DOWEL RODS, OR SECTIONS OF WIRE COAT HANGERS

HEAVY STRING

NEEDLE (DARNING TYPE, WITH LARGE EYE)

FELT-TIPPED MARKERS

GOLD TEMPERA PAINT

LARGE CARDBOARD BOX (FOR A SCREEN FRAME)

OLD BED SHEET (FOR A SCREEN)

MASKING TAPE

FLASHLIGHT (AS A LIGHT SOURCE)

PAPER FASTENERS

WHITE GLUE

CARBON PAPER (OPTIONAL)

DIRECTIONS for PUPPETS

1. PLAN A STORY FOR A PUPPET PLAY, AND DECIDE THE TYPE AND NUMBER OF CHARACTERS YOU WILL NEED. IT WOULD BE FUN TO WRITE A PLAY WITH SEVERAL OF YOUR FRIENDS, AND HAVE EACH MAKE A SET OF PUPPETS.

2. FOR EACH CHARACTER, DECIDE THE SIZE OF THE PUPPET YOU WANT TO MAKE. CUT THE BROWN PAPER BAG APART AT THE BACK SEAM, AND CUT OFF THE BOTTOM SECTION. OPEN AND FLATTEN THE PAPER.

3. CUT TWO PIECES OF PAPER FROM THE BAG LARGE ENOUGH ON WHICH TO DRAW THE FIGURE.

4. WITH WHITE GLUE, PASTE THE TWO PIECES OF BROWN PAPER TOGETHER.

5. SANDWICH THE GLUED PIECES BETWEEN NEWSPAPERS, AND PLACE A WEIGHT ON TOP TO PRESS THEM FLAT AS THEY DRY.

6. CONSIDER THE TYPE OF CHARACTER YOU PLAN TO PORTRAY AS YOU DESIGN THE PUPPET. ON PLAIN DRAWING PAPER, MAKE A SKETCH THE INTENDED SIZE OF THE PUPPET. COPY OR TRACE THE FIGURE OUTLINE ONTO THE PREPARED BROWN PAPER, DRAWING THE ARMS AND BODY SEPARATELY. USE CARBON PAPER OR COVER THE BACK OF YOUR DRAWING WITH PENCIL TO TRANSFER THE DESIGN.

HINGE HOLES

7. CUT OUT THE PUPPET. IF DESIRED, MAKE CUTS AND PERFORATIONS IN THE BODY WITH A UTILITY KNIFE OR PAPER PUNCHES. THESE CUTS WILL ALLOW LIGHT TO PASS THROUGH THE PUPPET AND WILL CREATE INTERESTING SHADOW PATTERNS. (TAKE APPROPRIATE SAFETY PRECAUTIONS WHEN WORKING WITH KNIVES AND OTHER SHARP TOOLS.) COLOR THE PUPPET, AND PUNCH HOLES IN THE SHOULDERS OF THE BODY AND IN THE ARMS.

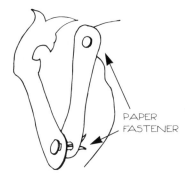

PAPER
FASTENER

8. ATTACH PAPER FASTENERS THROUGH THE HOLES AT THE SHOULDERS AND ELBOWS, LEAVING THEM LOOSE ENOUGH TO ALLOW PROPER MOVEMENT OF THE JOINTS.

9. FASTEN THE STRAIGHT STICKS OR RODS TO THE PUPPET'S HANDS AND BODY WITH GLUE OR BY SEWING THEM ON WITH HEAVY THREAD OR STRING. THE CENTRAL ROD SUPPORT SHOULD EXTEND FROM THE HEAD TO A FEW INCHES BELOW THE FOOT.

RODS ATTACHED
WITH STRING

DIRECTIONS FOR THE SCREEN

1. SELECT A LARGE CARDBOARD BOX. (GROCERY STORES OFTEN HAVE LARGE PACKING BOXES THAT ARE SUITABLE FOR THIS PURPOSE.)

2. CUT A SQUARE OPENING IN THE BOTTOM OF THE BOX, LEAVING A BORDER OF AT LEAST 2" ALL AROUND.

3. CUT A PIECE OF BED SHEET LARGE ENOUGH TO COVER THE OPENING, AND TAPE IT OVER THE OPENING ALONG THE INSIDE EDGES OF THE BOX.

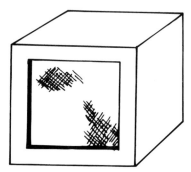

4. CUT A SLIT 2" WIDE IN THE
   FLOOR OF THE BOX, RUNNING
   THE WIDTH OF THE BOX.
   THIS IS FOR MOVING PUPPETS
   ACROSS THE SCREEN.

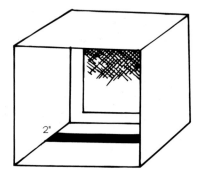

5. FOR LIGHTING THE SHADOW
   PLAY, TAPE A FLASHLIGHT TO
   THE INSIDE OF THE BOX BEHIND
   THE SCREEN, OR DIRECT A
   LAMP TOWARD THE SCREEN
   FROM THE BACK OF THE BOX.

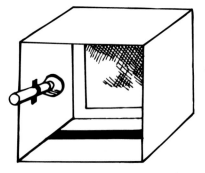

6. ADD MUSIC, AND CHOOSE SOMEONE TO ACT AS THE
   DALANG TO NARRATE YOUR STORY.

JAPANESE DECORATIVE PAPER

PAPER WAS INVENTED IN CHINA IN THE YEAR AD 105. THE FORMATION OF PAPER FIBER HAS UNDERGONE NO BASIC CHANGES IN ALMOST 2,000 YEARS. IN ABOUT AD 600, PAPERMAKING REACHED JAPAN. OF ALL THE DECORATIVE PAPERS PRODUCED AROUND THE WORLD TODAY, JAPAN STILL SUPPLIES THE GREATEST VARIETY OF TEXTURES. MOST JAPANESE PAPERS ARE DERIVED FROM THE BARK OF THE GAMPI, A TREE THAT GROWS WILD. THE GAMPI'S DARK OUTER BARK IS STRIPPED OFF, BOILED AND STEAMED, ALLOWING THE DARK BARK TO BE PARED AWAY FROM THE WHITE INNER BARK. THE WHITE INNER BARK FIBERS ARE SEPARATED, RINSED AND BEATEN ON A STONE SLAB WITH HARDWOOD CLUBS. THE RESULTING PULP IS PLACED IN VATS TO BE MADE INTO PAPER. RICE PAPER IS A MISNOMER, SINCE IT HAS NO RELATION TO RICE. JAPANESE PAPERS COMMONLY REFERRED TO AS RICE PAPER ARE MADE FROM KOZO, A MULBERRY PLANT.

DECORATED PAPERS ARE MADE ALL OVER THE WORLD USING MANY DIFFERENT TECHNIQUES. THEY RANGE IN PRICE FROM SEVERAL DOLLARS PER SHEET FOR GOLD EMBOSSED PAPERS TO A FEW PENNIES FOR EVERYDAY WRAPPING PAPER. BLOCK PRINTING AND MARBLING ARE TWO OF THE MOST COMMON TECHNIQUES USED FOR DECORATING PAPER.

MARBLING PRODUCES PATTERNS ON PAPER THAT SIMULATE MARBLE. THE PATTERNS ARE CREATED BY FLOATING DILUTED OIL-BASED PAINT ON A SOLUTION OF WATER AND SIZING (A THICKENER). DESIGNS ARE TRACED IN THE LAYER OF PAINT WITH A FINE POINT TOOL. A SHEET OF PAPER IS LOWERED ONTO THE SOLUTION, CAPTURING THE FLOATING DESIGN ON ITS SURFACE. MARBLING IS SOMETIMES USED ON THE EDGES OF ACCOUNT BOOKS AS A SECURITY MEASURE TO MAKE THE REMOVAL OF PAGES EASILY NOTICED.

BLOCK PRINTED PAPERS ARE MADE BY REPEATING PATTERNS ON PAPER WITH A BLOCK INTO WHICH A DESIGN HAS BEEN CARVED. MANY MATERIALS ARE USED FOR BLOCKS, SUCH AS WOOD, LINOLEUM, ERASERS AND POTATOES. THE CARVED BLOCKS ARE DIPPED IN PAINT OR BRUSHED WITH INK AND THEN PRESSED ONTO PAPER.

ANOTHER DECORATIVE TECHNIQUE IS EMBEDDING, IN WHICH ITEMS ARE PLACED BETWEEN TWO LAYERS OF WET PAPER. AS THE PAPER DRIES, IT SHRINKS AROUND THE OBJECTS AND HOLDS THEM IN PLACE, ASSUMING THE TEXTURE AND COLORS OF THE ITEMS SANDWICHED IN BETWEEN. DRIED LEAVES AND FLOWERS, COLORED THREADS AND SHAPES CUT FROM PAPER ARE FREQUENTLY USED.

BROWN BAG IDEA

MATERIALS AND TOOLS

TWO LARGE, PLAIN BROWN PAPER BAGS

CLEAR CONTACT PAPER, 18" WIDE

WHITE GLUE

ITEMS FOR EMBEDDING

SCISSORS

RULER

PENCIL

PAPER PUNCH

CLEAR TAPE

YARN OR BROWN TWINE

DIRECTIONS

1. THIS PROJECT WILL BE A DECORATED PAPER PORTFOLIO. DESIGN THE PORTFOLIO TO FIT YOUR NEEDS. ITS USE WILL DETERMINE THE DIMENSIONS AND THUS THE SIZE OF THE BROWN PAPER REQUIRED. THE PORTFOLIO FOR THIS PROJECT WAS DESIGNED TO HOLD 8 ½" X 11" PAPERS. CUT THE LARGE BROWN BAGS APART AT THE BACK SEAMS, AND CUT OFF THE BOTTOM SECTIONS.

2. FROM ONE OF THE BAGS, CUT A 14" X 20" PIECE OF PAPER FROM THE SECTION WITH THE FEWEST FOLDS. THIS WILL BECOME THE OUTSIDE COVER OF A FOLDER COVERED IN EMBEDDED DECORATIVE PAPER.

3. SELECT THE MATERIALS TO BE EMBEDDED AND ARRANGE THEM ON THE PAPER. POSSIBILITIES FOR EMBEDDING INCLUDE MAGAZINE CUTOUTS OF ANIMALS, FLOWERS, SPORTS FIGURES, CARTOON CHARACTERS, STAMPS, ETC., AND FLOWERS AND LEAVES DRIED BETWEEN THE PAGES OF MAGAZINES OR OLD TELEPHONE DIRECTORIES. MILKWEED SEEDS, FINE GRASS AND FIELD WEEDS CAN BE USED FOR LACE-LIKE EFFECTS. PUT A DAB OF GLUE UNDER EACH OBJECT TO HOLD IT IN PLACE. WHEN PLACING OBJECTS, REMEMBER THAT THE PAPER WILL BE FOLDED DOWN THE MIDDLE.

4. CUT A PIECE OF CONTACT PAPER LARGE ENOUGH TO COVER THE AREA OF THE DECORATED PAPER AND EXTEND AN INCH OR MORE BEYOND THE EDGE. (LEAVE THE BACKING PAPER ON THE CONTACT SHEET.) SELECT A WORKING SURFACE WITH A SMOOTH OR PLASTIC-LAMINATED TOP SO THAT THE EXPOSED EDGES OF THE CONTACT PAPER CAN BE PULLED UP EASILY FROM THE TABLE.

5. FROM THIS POINT ON, HAVE PEOPLE WORK IN TEAMS OF TWO TO PLACE THE CONTACT PAPER OVER THE DECORATED PAPER. CAREFULLY REMOVE THE BACKING PAPER FROM THE CONTACT SHEET. EACH PERSON, USING TWO HANDS (ONE HAND AT EACH CORNER), HOLDS THE

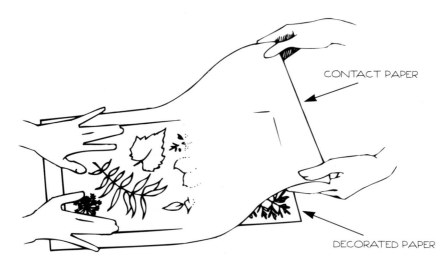

CONTACT PAPER

DECORATED PAPER

CONTACT PAPER OVER THE DECORATED PAPER. ONE PERSON LOWERS THE CONTACT PAPER, PLACING HIS OR HER END OF THE PAPER APPROXIMATELY 1" BEYOND THE BORDER OF THE BROWN PAPER, AND SLOWLY PRESSES DOWN A FEW INCHES AT A TIME. THE PERSON AT THE OPPOSITE END HOLDS THE CONTACT PAPER HIGH ENOUGH TO KEEP IT FROM STICKING TO THE WRONG PLACE OR TANGLING UP.

6. MITER THE CORNERS OF THE CONTACT PAPER (CUT OFF THE CORNERS AT 45-DEGREE ANGLES), AND FOLD THE EDGES OVER THE BROWN PAPER.

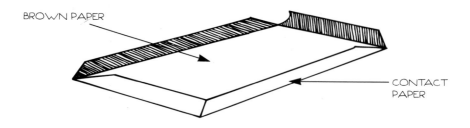

BROWN PAPER

CONTACT PAPER

7. FROM THE SECOND PREPARED BROWN PAPER BAG, CUT A PIECE OF PAPER 12" × 18" FOR THE LINING OF THE FOLDER.

8. PLACE THE 12" × 18" SHEET OVER THE BACK OF THE 14" × 20" SHEET THAT HAS BEEN COVERED WITH CONTACT PAPER. SECURE THE LINING PAPER TO THE BACK OF THE DECORATED PAPER WITH GLUE OR CLEAR TAPE.

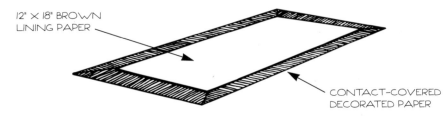

12" × 18" BROWN LINING PAPER

CONTACT-COVERED DECORATED PAPER

9. FOLD THE PORTFOLIO COVER IN HALF AND PUNCH ONE HOLE IN EACH SIDE CENTERED NEAR THE OUTSIDE EDGE. THREAD THE YARN OR TWINE THROUGH THE HOLES AND KNOT THEM ON THE INSIDE OF THE PORTFOLIO.

ISRAELI MARBLE MOSAICS

A MOSAIC IS A WORK INLAID WITH BITS OF MATERIALS THAT FORM A PATTERN OR PICTURE. THE SMALL PIECES THAT MAKE UP THE MOSAIC ARE CALLED TESSERAE. MOSAICS HAVE BEEN MADE FOR THOUSANDS OF YEARS. THEY REACHED THEIR PEAK AS A RELIGIOUS ART FORM DURING THE BYZANTINE PERIOD (AD 400–500). MOSAICS WERE INTRODUCED TO THE WESTERN WORLD FROM THE NEAR EAST DURING THE GOLDEN AGE OF GREECE AND ROME, WHERE THEY FLOURISHED AS AN IMPORTANT ART FORM. DUE TO THE PERMANENCY OF THE MATERIALS USED, MAINLY LIMESTONE AND MARBLE, MANY OF THE EARLY WORKS STILL EXIST.

MANY ANCIENT MOSAIC FLOORS HAVE BEEN DISCOVERED IN ISRAEL. THEY REVEAL MUCH INFORMATION ABOUT LIFE IN THAT COUNTRY FROM AD 50 TO AD 300, WHEN MOSAIC ART REACHED ITS ZENITH THERE. SKILLED ARTISANS WORKED ON

MOSAICS FOR TEMPLES AND PUBLIC BUILDINGS, CAREFULLY CUTTING AND FITTING HEAVY STONES TO FIT THE PICTURES THEY DESIGNED.

DURING THE EARLY PART OF THE TWENTIETH CENTURY IN ISRAEL, COOPERATIVE FARM COMMUNITIES KNOWN AS KIBBUTZIM WERE FORMED. ARTISANS LIVING ON KIBBUTZ EILON IN ISRAEL REVIVED THE ART OF THE MOSAIC. USING NATURAL MARBLE FROM THE LOCAL COUNTRYSIDE, THESE CRAFTSPEOPLE BROUGHT NEW LIFE TO THE HISTORY WHICH INSPIRED THEIR WORK. THEY ESTABLISHED A HOMOGENOUS DESIGN STYLE WITH A CHARACTER DISTINCTIVELY ISRAELI. THE TESSERAE WERE MADE OF MUTED EARTH-TONE CUBES OF MARBLE CALLED MARMI. TYPICAL NATURAL MARBLE TONES INCLUDE SOFT RUST, BROWN, GRAY, BUFF AND WHITE. DYED GRAVEL SERVED AS A BACKGROUND MATERIAL.

TODAY, MOSAICS MADE BY ARTISTS IN ISRAEL AND AROUND THE WORLD ARE NO LONGER CONFINED TO THE ORIGINAL CLASSIC MATERIALS SUCH AS MARBLE, LIMESTONE, CERAMIC, STONES AND GLASS BUT ARE FABRICATED FROM ALMOST EVERY CONCEIVABLE MATERIAL. THIS INCLUDES SEEDS, LEATHER, SHELLS, NAILS, CLOTH, WOOD, EGG SHELLS, FEATHERS, PASTA AND PAPER.

MOSAIC FROM KIBBUTZ EILON, ISRAEL.

THERE ARE TWO METHODS OF MAKING MOSAICS, THE DIRECT METHOD AND THE INDIRECT METHOD. IN THE DIRECT METHOD, THE TESSERAE ARE GLUED DIRECTLY TO THE PREPARED SURFACE. SPACES ARE LEFT BETWEEN THE TESSERAE TO ACCOMMODATE GROUT, A THIN MORTAR USED TO FILL IN THE CREVICES. THE GROUT IS ALLOWED TO DRY, OR SET, AND THE EXCESS GROUT IS REMOVED FROM THE SURFACE OF THE TESSERAE WITH A DAMP SPONGE OR CLOTH. IN THE INDIRECT METHOD, THE TESSERAE ARE GLUED TO A SHEET OF PAPER AND THEN PRESSED INTO AN ADHESIVE-COVERED SURFACE.

BROWN BAG IDEA

MATERIALS AND TOOLS

ONE OR TWO LARGE, PLAIN BROWN PAPER BAGS
(DEPENDING ON THE SIZE OF THE MOSAIC TO BE MADE)

WATERCOLOR PAINTS

ONE OR TWO BRUSHES

SCISSORS

GLUE

PENCIL

BLACK DRAWING INK

LIGHTWEIGHT CARDBOARD

DIRECTIONS

1. CUT THE BROWN BAGS APART AT THE BACK SEAMS, THEN CUT OFF THE BOTTOM SECTIONS.

2. DECIDE THE SIZE OF MOSAIC DESIRED AND CUT A SECTION THIS SIZE FROM THE PART OF ONE OF THE BAGS WITH THE FEWEST FOLDS OR CREASES.

3. PAINT THIS SECTION WITH BLACK INK FOR THE MOSAIC BACKGROUND.

4. DIVIDE THE REMAINING BROWN PAPER INTO LARGE SECTIONS AND PAINT EACH WITH ONE OF THE COLORS YOU WOULD LIKE FOR YOUR TESSERAE. THE BROWN PAPER MAY BE TINTED WITH A LIGHT WATERCOLOR WASH OF THE EARTH TONES COMMON TO KIBBUTZ EILON, OR YOU MAY PREFER MORE INTENSE COLORS. LET THE SECTIONS DRY.

5. CUT THE PAINTED SECTIONS INTO ½" SQUARES. (THE SIZE AND SHAPE OF THE TESSERAE MAY BE VARIED TO SUIT YOUR DESIGN.)

6. SEPARATE THE TESSERAE ACCORDING TO COLOR, AND PUT THEM IN SEPARATE CONTAINERS.

7. MAKE A LIGHT PENCIL SKETCH OF YOUR DESIGN ON THE PAINTED BACKGROUND PAPER.

8. FILL IN THE COMPOSITION WITH TESSERAE, GLUING AS YOU PROCEED AND BEING CAREFUL TO ALLOW A SMALL SPACE BETWEEN EACH TESSERAE TO SIMULATE THE AREA THAT WOULD BE GROUTED IN A TRADITIONAL MOSAIC.

9. MOUNT YOUR MOSAIC ON A PIECE OF LIGHTWEIGHT CARDBOARD APPROXIMATELY ½" LARGER THAN THE COMPLETED MOSAIC.

STRAW PLAQUE FROM BELORUSSIA.

EUROPE

ENGLISH KNIGHTS' SHIELDS   58

BELORUSSIAN STRAW PLAQUES   63

POLISH PAPER CUTS   66

ENGLISH KNIGHTS' SHIELDS

SHIELDS OF ARMOR HAVE BEEN USED FOR PROTECTION
THROUGHOUT HISTORY, IN ALL PARTS OF THE WORLD.
USUALLY CARRIED ON THE LEFT ARM, SHIELDS WERE USED BY
NATIVE AMERICAN TRIBES, AFRICAN TRIBES AND DURING THE
MIDDLE AGES IN EUROPE. SHIELDS WERE OFTEN DECORATED
WITH SYMBOLS THAT HAD SPECIAL SIGNIFICANCE TO THEIR
BEARERS.

IN ENGLAND DURING THE MIDDLE AGES, SHIELDS WERE USED
BY KNIGHTS TRAINED FOR MOUNTED COMBAT. KNIGHTS WERE
FOLLOWERS DEVOTED TO THE SERVICE OF A SUPERIOR,
USUALLY NOBILITY. AS SUCH, THEY WERE DESIGNATED TO
BEAR THE ARMS OR SYMBOLS REPRESENTING THEIR PATRON.
HERALDRY, THE TERM GIVEN TO THESE SYMBOLS OF PERSONAL
IDENTITY, MADE UP A NOBLE FAMILY'S COAT OF ARMS.

HERALDRY DEVELOPED AS A LANGUAGE FOR VISUALLY
COMMUNICATING THE BEARERS' IDENTITIES. IT IS A FORM OF

"PICTURE LANGUAGE," WITH PICTORIAL SYMBOLS REPRESENTING THE SUBJECTS BEING CONVEYED. PRESENT-DAY GRAPHIC DESIGNERS USE A FORM OF HERALDRIC ART WHEN CREATING TRADEMARKS, LOGOS, PATTERNS AND LABELS. THEY WORK WITH A LIMITED AMOUNT OF SPACE AND COLOR TO CONVEY SIMPLE FORMS AND CONTENT. BOOKPLATES, WHICH APPEAR WITH THE OWNERS' NAMES ON THE INSIDE COVERS OF SOME BOOKS, ARE ONE EXAMPLE OF PERSONAL HERALDRY. THEY ARE SIGNS OF OWNERSHIP, OFTEN IMPRINTED WITH THE WORDS "EX LIBRIS," WHICH IN LATIN MEANS "FROM THE LIBRARY OF." PLAYING CARDS ARE ALSO EXCELLENT EXAMPLES OF HERALDIC ART, INCORPORATING MANY OF THE ORNAMENTS USED IN THE MIDDLE AGES.

THE SHIELD, THE MOST IMPORTANT ELEMENT IN A COAT OF ARMS, DISPLAYS THE INSIGNIA OR SYMBOLS OF THE BEARER. THE AREA WITHIN THE SHIELD IS CALLED THE FIELD. THE SHIELD'S SURFACE IS DIVIDED INTO PARTS.

TYPES OF SHAPES

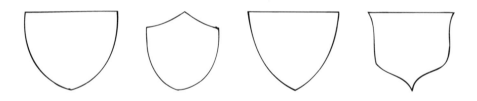

TYPES OF FIELD DIVISIONS

BROWN BAG IDEA

MATERIALS and TOOLS

    LARGE, PLAIN BROWN PAPER BAG

    TAGBOARD OR LIGHTWEIGHT CARDBOARD,
        APPROXIMATELY 14" X 18"

    CRAYONS, FELT-TIPPED MARKERS OR TEMPERA PAINT

    WHITE GLUE

    PENCIL

    SCISSORS

    STAPLER

    CARBON PAPER (OPTIONAL)

DIRECTIONS

1. CUT THE PAPER BAG APART AT THE BACK SEAM, AND CUT OFF THE BOTTOM SECTION.

2. FOLD THE BROWN PAPER IN HALF, AND CUT AT THE FOLD INTO TWO PIECES APPROXIMATELY 19" X 17".

3. PLACE THE TWO SECTIONS TOGETHER AND FOLD BOTH OF THEM IN HALF LENGTHWISE. DRAW THE SHAPE OF A SHIELD CENTERED ON THE FOLD AND CUT OUT TWO SHIELD SHAPES.

4. SELECT ONE SHIELD AND MEASURE AND DRAW A PENCIL LINE APPROXIMATELY 1 ½" IN FROM THE EDGE ALL THE WAY AROUND IT.

5. CUT ALONG THIS LINE. (THIS SHAPE WILL BE USED TO LAY OUT YOUR DESIGNS AND AS A TEMPLATE FOR A STURDY CARD-BOARD SHIELD SHAPE. FOR YOUNGER CHILDREN, FOUR BASIC SHIELD SHAPES COULD BE CUT FROM CARDBOARD TO BE USED AS TEMPLATES.)

6. PLACE THE SMALLER PAPER SHIELD ON THE CARDBOARD AND CUT THE CARDBOARD TO THE SAME SIZE.

7. PLACE THE CARDBOARD SHIELD ON THE LARGER BROWN PAPER SHIELD AND GLUE.

8. CUT 1 ½" SLITS APPROXIMATELY 1" APART ALONG THE EDGE OF THE PAPER BORDER. FOLD THE CUT EDGE OF THE BROWN PAPER SHIELD OVER THE CARDBOARD SHIELD AND GLUE.

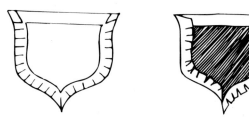

9. DESIGN AN ORIGINAL INSIGNIA. CAN YOU REPRESENT YOUR NAME USING A VISUAL SYMBOL? HAVE YOU ACCOMPLISHED SOMETHING THAT YOU ARE PROUD OF, SUCH AS REACHING A CERTAIN GOAL OR WINNING A PRIZE? ARE YOU A MEMBER OF A CLUB OR TEAM? CAN YOU DESIGN A SYMBOL THAT WOULD REPRESENT YOUR FAMILY'S BUSINESS OR OCCUPATION? DO YOU HAVE A FAVORITE ANIMAL OR PET? IN WHAT MONTH WERE YOU BORN? MAKE A LIST OF ALL THE POSSIBLE IDEAS, THEN TRY TO DESIGN SYMBOLS THAT BEST REPRESENT THEM.

10. PLAN YOUR DESIGN ON THE SMALLER PAPER SHIELD. DEPENDING ON THE NUMBER OF GRAPHIC SYMBOLS YOU CREATED, DIVIDE THE FIELD OF YOUR SHIELD INTO THE DESIRED NUMBER OF PARTS AND PROCEED TO PLACE THE SYMBOLS WITHIN EACH FIELD. TRANSFER THE DESIGNS TO THE SHIELD COMPLETED IN STEP 8. (USE CARBON PAPER OR RUB PENCIL LEAD OVER THE BACK OF THE DESIGN.)

11. COLOR IN THE DESIGNS ON THE MOUNTED SHIELD. REMEMBER THAT COLORS HAVE SYMBOLIC MEANINGS ALSO. WHAT DO DIFFERENT COLORS SUGGEST TO YOU? CAN YOU USE THIS INFORMATION TO ADD INTEREST TO YOUR DESIGN?

12. CUT A STRIP OF CARDBOARD APPROXIMATELY 2" X 12" FOR THE SHIELD'S HANDLE.

13. DRAW A LINE 1 ½" FROM EACH END.

14. FOLD UNDER AT THE LINES.

15. ATTACH THIS HANDLE TO THE BACK OF YOUR SHIELD WITH A STAPLER OR GLUE.

BELORUSSIAN STRAW PLAQUES

IN MANY PARTS OF THE WORLD, LIFE DEPENDED ON THE CROPS PLANTED BY THE FARMERS. THE FARMERS DEPENDED ON A FAVORABLE GROWING SEASON FOR THEIR HARVEST. IMAGES MADE OF STRAW AND OTHER SIMILAR MATERIALS WERE PLACED IN THE FIELDS AS OFFERINGS TO MOTHER NATURE WITH HOPES FOR A BOUNTIFUL YIELD. IN MEXICO, AMATE FIGURES MADE FROM BARK FIBERS WERE USED FOR THIS PURPOSE. IN BRITAIN, "CORN DOLLIES" AND, IN AMERICA, CORN HUSK DOLLS DEVELOPED IN A SIMILAR MANNER.

TODAY, STRAW AND CORNHUSKS ARE POPULAR MATERIALS FOR MANY CRAFT ITEMS THAT DECORATE OUR HOMES. STRAW IS AVAILABLE IN HOBBY SHOPS, FEED STORES AND STABLES. BEFORE IT IS SOLD, STRAW IS HARVESTED, CUT AND SPREAD OUT TO DRY FOR SEVERAL DAYS TO PREVENT MILDEW DURING STORAGE. IN PREPARATION FOR ITS USE IN CRAFTS, STRAW IS SOAKED IN WATER FOR A FEW HOURS, THEN WRAPPED IN

CLOTH. STRAW CAN BE USED AS A ROUND STALK OR SPLIT AND FLATTENED.

In MEXICO CITY, THERE ARE STILL A FEW CRAFTSMEN WHO MAKE PICTURES OUT OF A VERY THIN, ROUND, COMPACT BROOM STRAW CALLED PAPOTE. PAPOTE IS STAINED BY BOILING IT IN WATER CONTAINING DYES. THE ARTIST PLACES A DESIGN ON A PIECE OF PAPER, WHICH IS THEN COATED WITH A THIN LAYER OF BEESWAX. THE COLORED STRAWS, WHEN DRY, ARE PRESSED ONE-BY-ONE INTO THE WAX. THIS IS A PAINSTAKING ART, REQUIRING MUCH PATIENCE AND UNDERSTANDING.

In BELORUSSIA, LOCATED ALONG THE WESTERN BORDER OF THE FORMER U.S.S.R., A TRADITIONAL FORM OF ART USES FLAT STRAW. THE ROUND STALK IS SPLIT AND PRESSED FLAT WITH AN IRON. AT TIMES THE STRAW IS SCORCHED TO GIVE IT A MEDIUM-BROWN COLOR. THE SPLIT AND FLATTENED PIECES OF STRAW ARE USED TO MAKE MOSAIC-LIKE DESIGNS. THESE STRAW MARQUETRY PLAQUES POSSESS THE ORNAMENTAL STYLISTIC MOTIFS THAT ARE ESSENTIAL FEATURES OF EASTERN SLAVIC ART. THE STRAW PIECES ARE OFTEN ARRANGED IN GEOMETRIC DESIGNS ON THE DARK SURFACES OF WOODEN PANELS AND BOXES.

BROWN BAG IDEA

MATERIALS and TOOLS

RULER

SCISSORS OR SMALL PAPER CUTTER

PENCIL

LARGE, PLAIN BROWN PAPER BAG

WHITE GLUE

BLACK DRAWING INK

BRUSH

GRAPH PAPER (OPTIONAL)

DIRECTIONS

1. DECIDE THE SIZE OF YOUR PLAQUE AND CUT THE APPROPRIATE SIZE AND SHAPE FROM A BROWN BAG.

2. PAINT THE SURFACE OF THE SHAPE WITH BLACK INK. LET IT DRY.

3. FROM THE REMAINING PARTS OF THE PAPER BAG, CUT STRIPS OF VARYING WIDTHS AND LENGTHS.

4. PLAN YOUR DESIGN, POSSIBLY ON GRAPH PAPER, AND TRANSFER IT TO THE BLACK PAPER WITH PENCIL. EXPERIMENT WITH STYLIZED DESIGNS OF DIFFERENT SUBJECTS, INCLUDING PEOPLE, ANIMALS AND BUILDINGS. SINCE DELICATE DETAILS ARE HARD TO RENDER, TRY OUTLINING A GEOMETRIC DESIGN OF YOUR SUBJECT.

5. CAREFULLY START THE DESIGN BY PLACING THE STRIPS OF BROWN PAPER WITHIN THE OUTLINED BORDERS OF YOUR DESIGN, PARALLEL TO EACH OTHER AND TOUCHING. TRIM ANY OVERHANGING STRIPS TO FIT THE OUTLINE OF THE DESIGN. ONCE THE PIECES OF PAPER ARE ARRANGED IN THE APPROPRIATE PLACES, BRUSH THEM WITH GLUE AND SECURE IN PLACE.

6. ADD A BORDER AROUND THE EDGE OF THE PLAQUE WITH BROWN PAPER STRIPS.

BORDER DESIGNS

TRADITIONAL PLAQUE DESIGNS

POLISH PAPER CUTS

Wycinanki (pronounced vee-chee-<u>non</u>-kee) is the name given to intricate cut-paper designs from Poland. They were traditionally made during the Easter season to decorate the interior of Polish homes. The earliest tool used to cut the designs was sheep shears which even today is the tool of choice among many Polish paper cutters. Using this large, unwieldy cutting tool demands great skill and deftness. The designs are symmetrical, made by folding the paper before cutting. The oldest design motifs used are the spruce tree, the human figure and, most popular of all, the bird or rooster.

In the Kurpie district, north of Warsaw, paper cuts are made in a single color. These are called leluja (lee-<u>lew</u>-ya). These monochromatic cutouts featuring trees and birds are cut from a single sheet of paper folded lengthwise.

CIRCULAR, DOILY-TYPE CUTOUTS SIMILAR TO SNOWFLAKE DESIGNS FROM THE UNITED STATES ARE MADE IN BOTH THE KURPIE AND LOWICZ REGIONS OF POLAND. THESE ARE CALLED GWIAZDY (G-VEE-<u>OZ</u>-DAH), OR STARS. IN THE KURPIE REGION, THE GWIAZDY ARE CUT INTRICATELY FROM A SINGLE PIECE OF FOLDED PAPER. THIS TECHNIQUE PRODUCES A MONOCHROMATIC, LACE-LIKE PATTERN. IN THE LOWICZ REGION, THE GWIAZDY DESIGNS ARE FIRST CUT FROM BLACK PAPER. LAYERS OF COLORED PAPER ARE THEN PASTED ON TOP OF DIFFERENT SEGMENTS OF THE STAR. STYLIZED DESIGNS OF BUSHES OR SMALL TREES WITH UNFOLDING LEAVES AND FIGURES OF BIRDS OR ROOSTERS ARE COMMONLY USED.

TODAY THE PAPER CUTS ARE PRODUCED PRIMARILY FOR SALE TO TOURISTS. PATTERNS RANGE FROM TRADITIONAL GEOMETRIC COMPOSITIONS TO STYLIZED REPRESENTATIONS OF VILLAGE LIFE.

BROWN BAG IDEA

MATERIALS AND TOOLS

> LARGE, PLAIN BROWN PAPER BAG
>
> CHALK OR PENCIL
>
> GLUE
>
> SCISSORS
>
> SHEET OF WHITE OR COLORED PAPER FOR MOUNTING
> THE PAPER CUT

DIRECTIONS

1. CUT A SQUARE OR RECTANGULAR PIECE FROM THE BROWN PAPER BAG, AT LEAST 12" LONG ON EACH SIDE.

2. FOLD THE PAPER IN HALF.

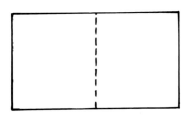 

3. WITH A PENCIL OR PIECE OF CHALK, OUTLINE ONE HALF OF YOUR DESIGN CENTERED ON THE FOLDED EDGE OF THE PAPER. REMEMBER THAT THE DESIGN SHOULD REMAIN AS ONE CONNECTED PIECE OF PAPER. IN ORDER TO INSURE THIS, YOUR PENCIL LINE SHOULD BE ONE CONTINUOUS LINE THAT NEVER CROSSES OVER ITSELF. TO HELP VISUALIZE THE DESIGN, LIGHTLY SHADE IN THE DESIGN AREA AND PERIODICALLY OPEN YOUR PAPER TO MAKE SURE THAT THE FOLDED EDGE REMAINS INTACT AND THAT THE DESIGN CONSISTS OF A SINGLE PIECE OF PAPER. REFOLD THE PAPER.

4. CUT ALONG THE CHALK OR PENCIL LINES WITH SCISSORS, AND UNFOLD.

5. GLUE THE DESIGN TO A PIECE OF WHITE OR COLORED PAPER.

POLISH PAPER CUT DESIGNS

MEXICO AND THE UNITED STATES

MEXICAN AMATE PAPER IMAGES   70

MEXICAN FOLK PAINTING   74

MEXICAN SERAPES   78

MEXICAN NEARIKAS   81

COLONIAL HEX SIGN QUILTS   84

MEXICAN AMATE
PAPER IMAGES

AMATE (AH-<u>MAH</u>-TAY) PAPER DATES BACK TO PRE-COLUMBIAN DAYS. IT IS SIMILAR TO TAPA CLOTH MADE IN THE PACIFIC ISLANDS AND TO AFRICAN BARK CLOTH.

AMATE PAPER IS MADE FROM THE BARK OF THE AMATE OR WILD FIG TREE BY THE OTOMI INDIANS OF SAN PABLITO, IN SOUTHERN MEXICO. STRIPS OF BARK ARE PEELED FROM THE TREE AND BOILED IN A WATER-AND-ASH SOLUTION. WHEN THE FIBERS ARE SUFFICIENTLY SOFTENED, THEY ARE PLACED ON A HARD SURFACE, CRISSCROSSED TO FORM SMALL SQUARES, THEN FELTED TOGETHER BY POUNDING WITH A STONE. THE RESULT IS A MESH-LIKE FABRIC.

VILLAGERS FASHION THIS PAPER INTO CUT-PAPER IMAGES. THE PAPER IS MADE IN BROWN AND WHITE. THE COLORS ARE RELATED TO RELIGIOUS AND MYSTICAL BELIEFS. DARK BROWN DENOTES HARMFUL SPELLS, WHILE LIGHT TAN OR WHITE DENOTES GOOD SPELLS. HOPING FOR GOOD CROPS AND

HEALTHY CATTLE, RITUAL FIGURES WERE CUT FROM AMATE PAPER TO INSURE AGRICULTURAL FERTILITY. SAN PABLITO IS THE ONLY PLACE IN MEXICO WHERE AMATE PAPER IS MADE USING PRE-HISPANIC TECHNIQUES. MOST OF THE PAPER IS SOLD IN THE TOWNS OF GUERRERO AND XALITLA, WHERE IT IS USED FOR PAINTINGS.

THE PAPER IMAGES ARE USUALLY SYMMETRICAL, WITH DESIGNS THAT ARE DECORATIVE INTERPRETATIONS OF PLANTS AND ANIMALS. SOME DESIGNS ARE FANCIFUL, REPRESENTING TWO- AND THREE-HEADED CREATURES WITH MANY ARMS AND LEGS AND AN ABUNDANCE OF PLUMAGE AND FOLIAGE.

BROWN BAG IDEA

MATERIALS AND TOOLS

> LARGE, PLAIN BROWN PAPER BAG
>
> PENCIL
>
> WAX PAPER
>
> PIECE OF WHITE PAPER FOR MOUNTING CUTOUT
>
> GLUE
>
> NEWSPAPER
>
> SCISSORS
>
> IRON
>
> SINK OR LARGE BOWL OF WATER

DIRECTIONS

1. PREPARE THE PAPER BAG TO SIMULATE A BARK-LIKE TEXTURE BY SOAKING IT IN WARM WATER FOR ABOUT TEN MINUTES. THIS LOOSENS THE GLUED SEAMS.

2. OPEN THE BAG AND CAREFULLY SQUEEZE OUT THE EXCESS WATER.

3. GENTLY SPREAD OUT THE BAG ON NEWSPAPER TO DRY. SOAKING AND CRUSHING THE PAPER, THEN SQUEEZING OUT THE WATER, WILL MAKE IT MORE PLIABLE. ANY TEARS THAT OCCUR DURING THE PROCESS CAN BE MENDED ON THE BACK WITH TAPE AFTER THE PAPER HAS DRIED.

4. PLACE THE DRY PAPER BETWEEN TWO PIECES OF WAX PAPER AND PRESS IT WITH A WARM IRON. REMEMBER TO PROTECT THE IRONING SURFACE WITH NEWSPAPER.

5. FOLD THE PAPER IN HALF WIDTHWISE. DRAW HALF OF YOUR DESIGN ON THE FOLDED PIECE OF BROWN PAPER, CENTERING YOUR DESIGN ON THE FOLDED EDGE. THE DESIGN SHOULD REMAIN AS ONE CONNECTED PIECE OF PAPER. IN ORDER TO INSURE THIS, THE OUTLINE OF YOUR DESIGN SHOULD BE ONE CONTINUOUS LINE THAT NEVER CROSSES OVER ITSELF.

6. WITH THE PAPER FOLDED, CUT OUT THE DESIGN.

FOLDED EDGE

7. OPEN THE FOLDED CUTOUT AND GLUE IT TO A PIECE OF WHITE BACKGROUND PAPER.

PAPER IMAGE MOTIFS

SPIRIT OF THE TOMATO

SPIRIT OF THE ORANGE

SPIRIT OF THE APPLE

SPIRIT OF THE BANANA

SPIRIT OF THE CHILE

SPIRIT OF THE PINEAPPLE

MEXICAN FOLK PAINTING

IN ADDITION TO ITS USE IN MEXICAN SYMBOLIC PAPER IMAGES, AMATE PAPER IS THE MATERIAL MOST OFTEN USED FOR MEXICO'S COLORFUL FOLK PAINTINGS. IT IS MADE IN SAN PABLITO BY THE OTOMI INDIANS. THE CRAFTSPEOPLE OF XALITLA, SKILLED IN DECORATING CERAMICS, PURCHASE THE PAPER FOR THEIR PAINTINGS. THE PAPER IS HANDMADE FROM THE BARK OF THE WILD FIG TREE.

PAINTING ON AMATE PAPER IS A FAIRLY NEW CRAFT, DATING BACK TO THE LATE 1950S. IT HAS BECOME THE PRIMARY SOURCE OF INCOME FOR THE ENTIRE COMMUNITY OF XALITLA, EMPLOYING BOTH CHILDREN AND ADULTS. AT FIRST, TRADITIONAL POTTERY DESIGNS CONSISTING OF FLORA AND FAUNA WERE PAINTED ON THE PAPER IN BRILLIANT, SOMETIMES FLUORESCENT COLORS. STYLIZED PLANTS AND ANIMALS WERE DEPICTED IN DECORATIVE COMPOSITIONS. EVENTUALLY, ARTISTS BEGAN TO DEVELOP A STYLE OF PICTORIAL ART WITH FIGURES AND SCENES REPRESENTING ACTIVITIES FROM THEIR DAILY LIVES,

INCLUDING FARMERS AT WORK, WEDDING SCENES AND FIESTAS. AZTEC MOTIFS WERE INTRODUCED. THE PAINTINGS REMAINED STYLIZED AND COLORFUL. VARIATIONS IN COLOR SCHEMES BEGAN TO BE USED, FROM BRILLIANT FLUORESCENTS, TO LIMITED PALETTES, SUCH AS BLACK AND WHITE OR JUST A BLACK OUTLINE.

TODAY, ARTISTS CONTINUE TO EXPERIMENT AND EXPAND THE ART FORM BY USING DIFFERENT SHAPES AND SIZES OF BARK PAPER. INDIVIDUAL ARTISTS ARE DEVELOPING THEIR OWN STYLES, MAKING THEIR PAINTINGS RECOGNIZABLE TO THE PUBLIC.

THE PEOPLE OF CONDEGA, NICARAGUA, IN CENTRAL AMERICA CREATE PAINTINGS VERY SIMILAR IN DESIGN AND COLOR TO THE EARLY MEXICAN FOLK PAINTINGS DONE ON AMATE PAPER. THE PAPER USED IN CONDEGA IS MADE FROM TUNO, THE BARK OF A PALM TREE. NICARAGUAN BARK PAPER IS MUCH THICKER AND MORE CLOTH-LIKE THAN AMATE PAPER. BAGS, BELTS, BOOK COVERS, TABLECLOTHS AND JACKETS ARE FASHIONED FROM THIS BARK CLOTH, THEN PAINTED AND SOLD IN CRAFT COOPERATIVES.

BROWN BAG IDEA

MATERIALS AND TOOLS

LARGE, PLAIN BROWN PAPER BAG

CRAYONS, TEMPERA PAINT OR FELT-TIPPED MARKERS

SCISSORS

SINK OR LARGE BOWL OF WATER

DIRECTIONS

1. PREPARE THE PAPER BAG TO SIMULATE A CLOTH-LIKE TEXTURE BY SOAKING IT IN WATER FOR ABOUT TEN MINUTES. THIS LOOSENS THE GLUED SEAMS.

2. OPEN THE BAG AND CAREFULLY SQUEEZE OUT THE EXCESS WATER.

3. GENTLY SPREAD OUT THE BAG ON NEWSPAPER TO DRY. SOAKING AND CRUSHING THE PAPER, THEN SQUEEZING OUT THE WATER, WILL MAKE IT MORE PLIABLE. ANY TEARS THAT

OCCUR DURING THE PROCESS CAN BE MENDED ON THE BACK WITH TAPE AFTER THE PAPER HAS DRIED.

4. DECIDE THE SIZE OF YOUR PAINTING. A 12" X 18" PIECE IS GOOD TO WORK WITH.

5. AFTER THE PAPER IS DRY, TRIM IT TO THE PROPER SIZE AND ROUND THE CORNERS WITH SCISSORS.

6. PLAN THE TYPE OF DESIGN YOU WOULD LIKE, AND SKETCH THE BASIC OUTLINE ON THE PAPER.

7. OUTLINE THE FIGURES IN YOUR DESIGN WITH A BLACK FELT-TIPPED MARKER OR CRAYON.

8. FILL IN THE OUTLINED DESIGNS WITH COLORS, USING TEMPERA PAINT, CRAYONS OR FELT-TIPPED MARKERS. REMEMBER: THE DESIGN SHOULD BE BRIGHT, COLORFUL AND DECORATIVE.

AZTEC SYMBOLS

FOLK PAINTING DESIGNS

FLORA AND FAUNA

ANCIENT AZTEC

PICTORIAL

MEXICAN SERAPES

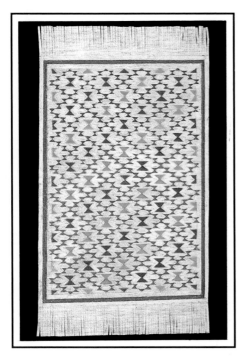

The serape (SEH-<u>RAH</u>-PAY) IS ONE OF THE FINEST EXAMPLES OF THE WEAVER'S CRAFT IN MEXICO. THE TRADITIONAL SERAPE IS A WOOLEN BLANKET WORN ONLY BY MEN. IT HAS MANY USES. WITH A SLIT IN THE CENTER, IT IS WORN OVER THE BODY FOR WARMTH, DRAPED OVER THE SHOULDER FOR DECORATION, AS A WEDDING CLOAK AND, FINALLY, AS A SHROUD. WITHOUT SLITS, SERAPES ARE USED AS RUGS, BLANKETS, BEDSPREADS OR WALL HANGINGS.

The CRAFT OF WEAVING SERAPES BEGAN IN THE TOWN OF SAN MIGUEL DE ALLENDE IN THE EIGHTEENTH CENTURY THE PATTERNED DESIGNS ARE A MIXTURE OF INDIAN, SPANISH AND MOORISH INFLUENCE. THEY ARE GEOMETRIC, MADE OF INTERLOCKING DIAMONDS, ZIGZAGS AND VARIATIONS OF TRIANGLES AND POLYGONS. BRIGHTLY STRIPED SERAPES ARE STILL PRODUCED IN SALTILLO, THE CAPITAL OF THE MEXICAN STATE COAHUILA. PATTERNS UTILIZING BIRDS, DUCKS AND FISH

ON SOLID BACKGROUNDS HAVE COME INTO USE ONLY WITHIN THE LAST THIRTY YEARS.

TRADITIONAL WEAVERS USED DYES MADE FROM NATURAL ELEMENTS IN THE ENVIRONMENT TO ADD COLOR TO THEIR SERAPES. BOILING THE COCHINEAL, A PARASITIC INSECT, PRODUCED A BRILLIANT SCARLET COLOR. BLACK WAS MADE FROM THE SEED OF A TROPICAL TREE, WHILE PURPLE WAS OBTAINED FROM MOLLUSK SHELLS. TODAY'S COLORS ARE MADE FROM ANILINE DYES IMPORTED FROM THE UNITED STATES. SOME SERAPES ARE MADE IN GARISH COLORS. OTHERS ARE MADE IN SUBDUED, NATURAL COLORS AND ARE MORE DIFFICULT TO FIND.

SERAPES ARE MADE FROM WOOL WHICH IS DYED, SEPARATED ACCORDING TO COLOR, THEN WASHED, CARDED, SPUN AND WOUND INTO SKEINS. THE WARP THREADS ARE MADE OF HEAVY COTTON STRING.

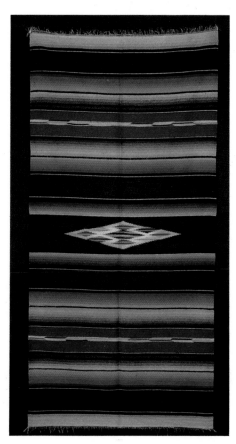

SERAPE FROM SALTILLO, MEXICO.

BROWN BAG IDEA

MATERIALS and TOOLS

LARGE, PLAIN BROWN PAPER BAG

CRAYONS, TEMPERA PAINT OR FELT-TIPPED MARKERS

PENCIL

SCISSORS

SINK OR LARGE BOWL OF WATER

RULER

DIRECTIONS

1. PREPARE THE PAPER BAG TO SIMULATE A CLOTH-LIKE TEXTURE BY SOAKING IT IN WATER FOR ABOUT TEN MINUTES. THIS LOOSENS THE GLUED SEAMS.

2. OPEN THE BAG AND CAREFULLY SQUEEZE OUT THE EXCESS WATER.

3. GENTLY SPREAD OUT THE BAG ON NEWSPAPER TO DRY. SOAKING AND CRUSHING THE PAPER, THEN SQUEEZING OUT THE WATER, WILL MAKE IT MORE PLIABLE. ANY TEARS THAT OCCUR DURING THE PROCESS CAN BE MENDED ON THE BACK WITH TAPE AFTER THE PAPER HAS DRIED.

4. PLAN A DESIGN AND SKETCH IT ON THE PAPER WITH PENCIL. USE A RULER IF YOU PLAN TO MAKE A GEOMETRIC PATTERN. FOR LOOSER DESIGNS, FREEHAND SKETCHING IS FINE. IF YOU WOULD LIKE FRINGE, ALLOW 2" TO 3" AT EITHER END OF THE DESIGN.

5. ADD COLOR TO THE DESIGN WITH CRAYONS, TEMPERA PAINT OR FELT-TIPPED MARKERS.

6. FOR FRINGE, MARK ½" INTERVALS ON THE BOTTOM AND TOP BORDERS. CUT FROM THOSE POINTS UP TO THE PERIMETERS OF THE DESIGN.

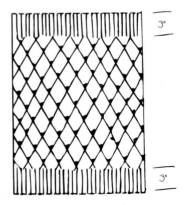

MEXICAN NEARIKAS

THE HUICHOL INDIAN PEOPLE LIVE IN THE JALISCO AND NAYARIT REGIONS OF MEXICO, ON THE PEAKS OF THE SIERRA MADRE MOUNTAINS. FOR THE HUICHOLES, ART IS FUNCTIONAL AS WELL AS DECORATIVE. IT IS MEANT TO ASSURE THE HEALTH AND FERTILITY OF CROPS, ANIMALS AND PEOPLE. HUICHOL DESIGNS COME FROM THE PEOPLE'S HISTORY, RELIGION AND DREAMS. MOST HUICHOL ADULTS ARE INVOLVED IN THE PRODUCTION OF SOME FORM OF SACRED ART AT SOME TIME IN THEIR LIVES, MAKING YARN CROSSES, DECORATING GOURDS WITH YARN OR BEADS OR MAKING NEARIKAS.

THE NEARIKA (NEER-EE-KAH), ONE OF THE MOST STRIKING, COLORFUL CRAFTS OF MEXICO, IS A PAINTING MADE WITH YARN. THE WORD NEARIKA CAN BE UNDERSTOOD TO MEAN LIKENESS, FACE, ASPECT, IMAGE, REPRESENTATION, EMBLEM OR, SIMPLY, PICTURE. IT IS ALSO THE TERM USED TO DESCRIBE THIS SPECIFIC TYPE OF MODERN FOLK PAINTING. NEARIKAS ARE A FORM OF SACRED ART AND STORY-TELLING, A MEANS OF

RECORDING IN TWO-DIMENSIONAL FORM EVENTS THAT ARE MYTHS TO SOME BUT TRUE RELIGIOUS HISTORY TO OTHERS.

YARN PAINTINGS ARE MADE BY PRESSING FINE YARN INTO BEESWAX THAT HAS BEEN APPLIED TO A SHEET OF THIN PLYWOOD. BEESWAX SOFTENED BY THE SUN'S HEAT IS SPREAD EVENLY OVER A WOODEN BOARD. A DESIGN IS SCRATCHED IN THE WAX WITH A SHARP INSTRUMENT. SPACES ARE FILLED IN BY PRESSING YARN DOWN FIRMLY INTO THE WAX.

ONE OF THE UNIQUE ASPECTS OF THE NEARIKA IS THE TECHNIQUE USED TO APPLY THE YARN TO THE BEESWAX, WHICH ACHIEVES A SPECIFIC PATTERN AND TEXTURE. MOST ARTISTS PUT ONE TO THREE COLORS OF YARN AROUND THE NEARIKA'S EDGE TO MAKE A BORDER. NEXT, THEY OUTLINE THE SHAPES IN THEIR DESIGNS. THE THIRD STEP INVOLVES FILLING IN EACH OF THE SHAPES OF THE DESIGN USING ONE CONTINUOUS PIECE OF YARN. FINALLY, THE PICTURE'S BACKGROUND IS COMPLETED USING THE SAME TECHNIQUE.

BROWN BAG IDEA

MATERIALS AND TOOLS

LARGE, PLAIN BROWN PAPER BAG

FELT-TIPPED MARKERS (FINE-TIPPED FOR DRAWINGS 9" × 12" OR THICKER FOR DRAWINGS 12" × 18") OR CRAYONS

PIECE OF CONSTRUCTION PAPER OR CARDBOARD

SCISSORS

GLUE

DIRECTIONS

1. CUT THE PAPER BAG APART AT THE BACK SEAM, AND CUT OFF THE BOTTOM SECTION.

2. CUT OUT A PIECE OF PAPER FOR YOUR NEARIKA, EITHER 9" × 12" OR 12" × 18".

3. PLAN YOUR DESIGN CAREFULLY, KEEPING IN MIND THAT THE PAINTING SHOULD TELL A STORY AND INCLUDE THE MOST IMPORTANT CHARACTERS.

4. WITH A PENCIL, OUTLINE VERY LIGHTLY THE OBJECTS IN YOUR PICTURE ON THE BROWN PAPER.

5. WITH A FELT-TIPPED MARKER OR CRAYON FOR EACH COLOR, OUTLINE EACH FIGURE AND THE BORDER IN YOUR COMPOSITION.

6. SELECT A FELT-TIPPED MARKER OR CRAYON AND BEGIN FILLING IN THE OUTLINED FORMS. DRAW THE LINES AS IF THEY WERE SINGLE, LONG PIECES OF YARN, NOT LIFTING YOUR HAND UNTIL YOU HAVE FILLED IN EACH SPACE AS MUCH AS POSSIBLE WITHOUT OVERLAPPING LINES. USE A VARIETY OF BRILLIANT, CONTRASTING COLORS IN THE FIGURES AND THE BACKGROUND TO CREATE A DYNAMIC AND INTERESTING COMPOSITION.

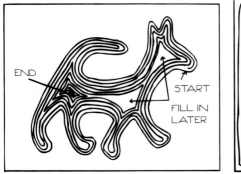

END

START

FILL IN LATER

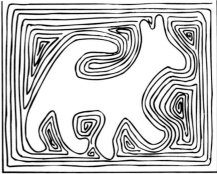

7. AFTER FILLING IN THE FIGURES IN YOUR PICTURE, FILL IN THE BACKGROUND USING THE SAME TECHNIQUE. YOU MAY HAVE TO STOP AND START YOUR LINES SEVERAL TIMES IF YOU RUN OUT OF SPACE IN A PARTICULAR AREA. ARE THE COLORS BRIGHT WITH CONTRAST? CAN YOUR FRIENDS INTERPRET THE STORY PORTRAYED IN YOUR PAINTING?

COLONIAL HEX SIGN QUILTS

In THE HILLS AND MOUNTAINS OF SOUTHEASTERN PENN-
SYLVANIA LIVE THE PEOPLE KNOWN AS THE PENNSYLVANIA
DUTCH, DESCENDANTS OF GERMAN AND SWISS REFUGEES
WHO CAME TO AMERICA SEEKING RELIGIOUS FREEDOM. THEIR
ANCESTORS ESTABLISHED MANY LUSH FARMS. THEIR BARNS,
TYPICALLY PAINTED RED, ARE OFTEN DECORATED WITH
COLORFUL GEOMETRIC DESIGNS AND SYMBOLS, WHICH HAVE
BECOME A TRADEMARK OF THE PENNSYLVANIA DUTCH AND
THE FOLK ART OF PENNSYLVANIA.

During THE LATE NINETEENTH CENTURY, THESE SIGNS WERE
KNOWN AS EARLY AMERICAN HEX SIGNS. POPULAR FOLKLORE
ASSOCIATES THESE SIGNS WITH SUPERSTITIONS, ALTHOUGH
MANY DIFFERENT OPINIONS CONCERNING THEIR MEANING EXIST.
HEX SIGNS ARE ALSO DRAWN AND PAINTED FOR PURELY
DECORATIVE PURPOSES. MANY OF THESE DESIGNS INCLUDE THE
FORMS OF THE MOON, SUN AND STARS AS WELL AS SYMBOLS
OF FERTILITY AND LIFE. THE STAR DESIGNS RANGE FROM FIVE-

POINTED STARS TO SOME WITH AS MANY AS THIRTY-TWO POINTS. MANY UNUSUAL HEX SIGN DESIGNS FEATURE UNICORNS, ROOSTERS, PEACOCKS AND HORSES, IN ALL SIZES, READY TO MOUNT. THESE DESIGNS ARE SOLD THROUGHOUT THE COUNTRY AS BARN AND HOME DECORATIONS.

HEX SIGNS ARE SIMILAR IN COLOR AND DESIGN TO EARLY QUILT DESIGNS. THERE ARE TWO MAJOR TYPES OF QUILT DESIGNS, PIECED AND APPLIQUE'. PIECED QUILTS, MOST FREQUENTLY REFERRED TO AS PATCHWORK QUILTS, ARE MADE BY SEWING TOGETHER SMALL PIECES OF FABRIC TO FORM AN OVERALL PATTERN. APPLIQUE' QUILTS ARE MADE BY STITCHING TOGETHER FABRIC BLOCKS, EACH CREATED BY SEWING A DESIGN CUT FROM ONE FABRIC TO ANOTHER BACKGROUND BLOCK OF FABRIC.

MANY OF THE STAR DESIGNS FOUND ON BARNS ARE ALSO USED BY QUILTERS AND GIVEN "QUILTING" NAMES. THE SIX-POINTED STAR IS CALLED THE EVENING STAR, THE TRIPLE-POINTED STAR IS KNOWN AS THE CARPENTER'S WHEEL AND THE EIGHT-POINTED STAR IS CALLED THE STAR OF LEMOYNE. QUILT DESIGNS ALSO FEATURE A VARIETY OF SUN PATTERNS SIMILAR IN STYLE TO THOSE OF HEX SIGNS.

BROWN BAG IDEA

MATERIALS AND TOOLS

TWO LARGE, PLAIN BROWN PAPER BAGS

RED TEMPERA PAINT

FELT-TIPPED MARKERS OR CRAYONS

RULER

COMPASS

SCISSORS

PENCIL

GLUE

BRUSH

DIRECTIONS

1. GIVE ONE OF THE PAPER BAGS A CLOTH-LIKE TEXTURE BY SOAKING IT IN WATER FOR ABOUT TEN MINUTES. THIS LOOSENS THE GLUED SEAMS.

2. OPEN THE BAG AND CAREFULLY SQUEEZE OUT THE EXCESS WATER.

3. GENTLY SPREAD OUT THE BAG ON NEWSPAPER TO DRY. SOAKING AND CRUSHING THE PAPER, THEN SQUEEZING OUT THE WATER, WILL MAKE IT MORE PLIABLE. ANY TEARS THAT OCCUR DURING THE PROCESS CAN BE MENDED ON THE BACK WITH TAPE AFTER THE PAPER HAS DRIED.

4. THIN THE RED TEMPERA PAINT WITH WATER, AND PAINT THE PREPARED PAPER.

5. CUT THE SECOND BROWN BAG APART AT THE BACK SEAM, AND CUT OFF THE BOTTOM SECTION.

6. WITH A RULER, MEASURE THE SECOND BAG INTO 5 ½" SQUARES. (THIS SHOULD GIVE YOU APPROXIMATELY EIGHTEEN SQUARES FOR THE QUILT DESIGNS.)

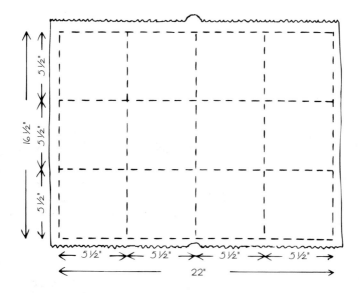

7. WITH A COMPASS AND RULER, CREATE DESIGNS ON THE SQUARES USING A COMBINATION OF BOTH QUILT AND HEX SIGN PATTERNS. COLOR THE DESIGNS WITH FELT-TIPPED MARKERS OR CRAYONS.

8. GLUE THE COMPLETED SQUARES AT EVENLY SPACED INTERVALS ON THE RED BACKGROUND. TWELVE TO FIFTEEN DESIGNS SHOULD FIT.

HEX SYMBOLS

EIGHT-POINTED STAR

FLOWER STAR

FIVE-POINTED STAR

SIXTEEN-POINTED
STAR

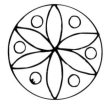

SIX-LOBED
PETAL STAR

DOUBLE STAR

QUILT DESIGNS

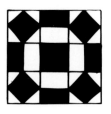

ROLLING STONE

WHEEL OF
FORTUNE

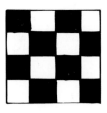

PATCH QUILT

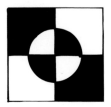

ROB PETER TO
PAY PAUL

WRENCH QUILT

EIGHT-POINTED STAR
OR VARIABLE QUILT
STAR

PLAINS INDIAN BUFFALO SHIELD.

NATIVE AMERICA

MOCCASINS   90

PARFLECHE   94

SHIELDS   98

RAWHIDE VESTS   102

KACHINAS   106

SCROLLS   110

THUNDERBIRD RUGS   114

BONE BREASTPLATES   119

PAINTED BUFFALO ROBES   124

MOCCASINS

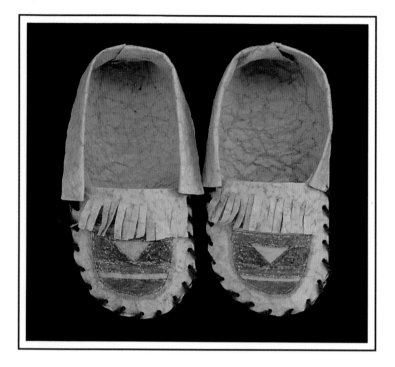

Moccasins were the most typical form of footwear worn by Native North Americans. There were many different styles. Forest moccasins were made of thin buckskin leather. They were soft and flexible to wear, dried easily and served well for walking in damp canoes and over slippery rocks or fallen trees. Forest moccasins were used by the Eastern Woodland tribes. The sole and upper parts of each shoe were made from one piece of leather, with seams at the instep and heel. Decorative beadwork was attached to the top of the moccasin in floral designs. The word "tenderfoot" was used to describe the early pioneers whose feet were too tender to wear these buckskin moccasins because they were accustomed to wearing hard-soled shoes.

Prairie moccasins, worn by the Plains and Southwest Indians, consisted of thick, rawhide soles, sewn to soft

LEATHER UPPER PARTS. THESE WERE USEFUL IN PROTECTING FEET FROM STONES, ROCKS AND DESERT CACTI. FOR WINTER, THE MOCCASINS WERE MADE A BIT LARGER TO ACCOMMODATE FUR OR CLOTH LININGS. BEADS AND PORCUPINE QUILLS IN CHARACTERISTIC GEOMETRIC DESIGNS ADORNED THE TOPS OF PRAIRIE MOCCASINS.

BROWN BAG IDEA

MATERIALS and TOOLS

TWO LARGE, PLAIN BROWN PAPER BAGS

PENCIL

WHITE GLUE

CRAYONS

YARN

RULER

SCISSORS

NEEDLE (DARNING TYPE, WITH A LARGE EYE)

PAPER PUNCH (⅛" IF AVAILABLE)

SINK OR LARGE BOWL OF WATER

DIRECTIONS

1. PREPARE THE PAPER BAGS TO SIMULATE A LEATHER TEXTURE BY SOAKING THEM IN WATER FOR ABOUT TEN MINUTES. THIS LOOSENS THE GLUED SEAMS.

2. OPEN THE BAGS AND CAREFULLY SQUEEZE OUT THE EXCESS WATER.

3. GENTLY SPREAD OUT THE BAGS ON NEWSPAPER TO DRY. SOAKING AND CRUSHING THE PAPER, THEN SQUEEZING OUT THE WATER, WILL MAKE IT MORE PLIABLE. ANY TEARS THAT OCCUR DURING THE PROCESS CAN BE MENDED ON THE BACK WITH TAPE AFTER THE PAPER HAS DRIED.

4. GLUE THE DRIED PAPER PIECES ON TOP OF EACH OTHER TO FORM A SINGLE, TWO-LAYER, STRONG SHEET.

5. CUT THE DOUBLE-THICK SHEET IN HALF.

6. FOLD EACH PIECE IN HALF.

7. PLACE YOUR RIGHT FOOT ON ONE HALF OF THE PAPER, INSTEP RUNNING PARALLEL WITH THE FOLD, ABOUT ¾" FROM THE FOLDED EDGE. DRAW A LINE, LEAVING A ¾" MARGIN ALL AROUND YOUR FOOT <u>EXCEPT AT THE HEEL</u>, WHERE YOU SHOULD LEAVE 1". REPEAT THE PROCESS FOR THE LEFT FOOT, PLACING IT ABOUT ¾" FROM THE FOLDED EDGE.

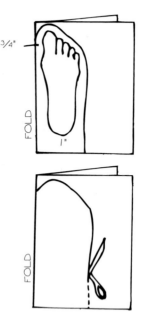

8. CUT ALONG THE LINE, LEAVING THE FOLDED EDGE INTACT. SAVE ALL PAPER SCRAPS FOR LATER USE.

9. OPEN BOTH PIECES TO PREPARE FOR DESIGN AND CUTTING. NOTE THE SHADED PORTIONS OF THE ACCOMPANYING ILLUSTRATION, INDICATING AREAS APPROPRIATE FOR ADDING DESIGNS. USE CRAYONS TO ADD COLOR AND INTEREST IN THESE AREAS. YOU MAY CHOOSE TO CREATE FLORAL DESIGNS, AS THE EASTERN WOODLAND TRIBES DID ON THEIR MOCCASINS, OR YOU MAY CHOOSE A MORE GEOMETRIC PATTERN, COMMON TO PRAIRIE MOCCASINS.

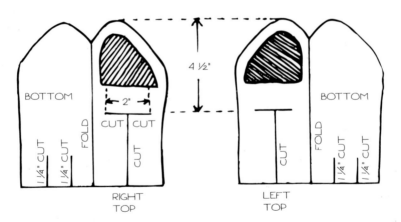

10. MEASURE AND LIGHTLY PENCIL IN THE CUTTING LINES, AS INDICATED IN THE ILLUSTRATION. CUT ALONG THE MEASURED LINES ON BOTH MOCCASINS.

11. REFOLD EACH MOCCASIN AND, WITH YARN, STITCH AROUND THE FRONT AND SIDE EDGES AS INDICATED IN THE ILLUSTRATION. HOLES MADE WITH A PAPER PUNCH THROUGH BOTH HALVES OF EACH MOCCASIN MAKE STITCHING EASIER. HOLES SHOULD BE ABOUT ½" APART.

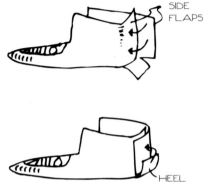

SIDE FLAPS

HEEL FLAP

12. LIFT THE TOP FLAPS TO OPEN THE MOCCASIN. AT THE HEEL OF EACH MOCCASIN, FOLD IN THE SIDE FLAPS, OVERLAPPING THE FLAPS TO MAKE A HEEL. GLUE THE FLAPS TOGETHER AND LET DRY.

13. LIFT UP THE REMAINING HEEL FLAP AND GLUE TO THE BACK OF THE MOCCASIN.

CUFFS

14. THE HEEL AND SIDES OF THE MOCCASIN ARE FOLDED OVER TO MAKE A CUFF.

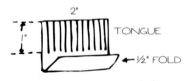

2"

1"

TONGUE

← ½" FOLD

15. TO CREATE THE MOCCASINS' TONGUES, CUT OUT TWO 2" X 2" PIECES OF PAPER FROM THE RESERVED PAPER SCRAPS. AT ONE EDGE OF EACH PIECE, CUT ONE-INCH-LONG FRINGE. AT THE OPPOSITE EDGE OF EACH PIECE, FOLD UNDER ½" OF THE PAPER.

GLUE FLAP TO UNDERSIDE

16. GLUE THE ½" FOLDED EDGE OF EACH TONGUE TO THE UNDERSIDE OF EACH MOCCASIN.

17. TO CREATE A DRAWSTRING, RUN A PIECE OF YARN AROUND THE TOP OF THE MOCCASIN, UNDER THE CUFF. MAKE A BOW.

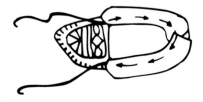

PARFLECHE

THE PARFLECHE WAS A TYPE OF CARRYING CASE USED
BY THE PLAINS INDIANS. THE NAME IS FRENCH IN ORIGIN AND
WAS USED AS EARLY AS 1700 TO MEAN RAWHIDE ARTICLES.
PARFLECHES WERE MADE OF RECTANGULAR PIECES OF
RAWHIDE. THEY RANGED IN SIZE FROM ONE TO THREE FEET
LONG AND SIX TO EIGHTEEN INCHES WIDE. THERE WERE ALSO
MINIATURE, POCKET-SIZE PARFLECHES. THEY WERE USED TO
CARRY SUCH THINGS AS CLOTHING AND DRIED FOODS.

THE PARFLECHE WAS AN ENVELOPE MADE BY FIRST FOLDING
IN THE SIDES AND THEN THE ENDS OF THE RAWHIDE. HOLES
WERE PUNCHED IN THE ENDS OF THE RAWHIDE. LEATHER
THONGS WERE LACED THROUGH THE HOLES TO TIE THE ENDS
TOGETHER. DESIGNS WERE PAINTED ON THE PARFLECHES BY
WOMEN OF THE TRIBE. THESE DESIGNS CONSISTED OF SIMPLE,
BOLD GEOMETRIC SHAPES EXECUTED IN BRIGHT COLORS—
USUALLY RED, BLACK, YELLOW AND GREEN.

BROWN BAG IDEA

MATERIALS AND TOOLS

TWO LARGE, PLAIN BROWN PAPER BAGS

PENCIL

WHITE GLUE

CRAYONS

STRING

RULER

SCISSORS

PAPER PUNCH, NAIL OR LARGE NEEDLE

SINK OR LARGE BOWL OF WATER

DIRECTIONS

1. PREPARE THE PAPER BAGS TO SIMULATE A LEATHER TEXTURE BY SOAKING THEM IN WATER FOR ABOUT TEN MINUTES. THIS LOOSENS THE GLUED SEAMS.

2. OPEN THE BAGS AND CAREFULLY SQUEEZE OUT THE EXCESS WATER.

3. GENTLY SPREAD OUT THE BAGS ON NEWSPAPER TO DRY. SOAKING AND CRUSHING THE PAPER, THEN SQUEEZING OUT THE WATER, WILL MAKE IT MORE PLIABLE. ANY TEARS THAT OCCUR DURING THE PROCESS CAN BE MENDED ON THE BACK WITH TAPE AFTER THE PAPER HAS DRIED.

4. GLUE THE DRIED PAPER PIECES ON TOP OF EACH OTHER TO FORM A SINGLE, TWO-LAYER, STRONG SHEET.

5. MEASURE AND CUT A RECTANGLE THAT MEASURES 27" × 18". ROUND THE CORNERS WITH SCISSORS.

6. MARK AND FOLD THE PAPER ACCORDING TO THE MEASUREMENTS INDICATED IN THE ILLUSTRATION. FOLD AND CREASE ALONG THE DOTTED LINES, FOLDING IN THE OVER-LAPPING TOP AND BOTTOM EDGES FIRST.

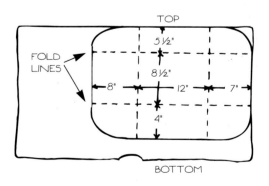

7. FOLD IN THE SIDES, AND YOU CAN SEE YOUR ENVELOPE TAKE SHAPE. REOPEN THE BAG AND TURN IT OVER ON THE TABLE TO DECORATE THE OUTSIDE OF THE PARFLECHE.

8. THE AREA YOU WILL DESIGN IS NEATLY OUTLINED BY THE CREASED FOLD MARKS. USE A PENCIL OR BLACK CRAYON TO PLAN THE OUTLINE OF YOUR DESIGN. BEGIN ADDING COLOR TO THE DESIGN WITH CRAYONS, PRESSING HARD FOR STRONG COLORS.

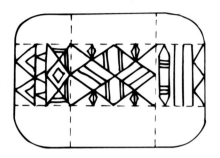

9. REFOLD YOUR PARFLECHE AND PUNCH HOLES IN THE CORNERS, AS INDICATED IN THE ILLUSTRATION. BE SURE TO PUNCH THE HOLES THROUGH BOTH LAYERS OF THE PAPER.

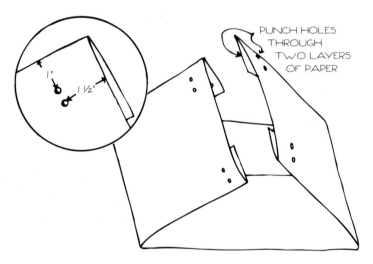

PUNCH HOLES THROUGH TWO LAYERS OF PAPER

1"

1 ½"

10. LACE STRING THROUGH THE HOLES ON EACH SIDE OF THE PARFLECHE TO FASTEN THE SIDES TOGETHER. USE ONE PIECE OF STRING FOR EACH SIDE TO THREAD THROUGH THE OVERLAPPING HOLES.

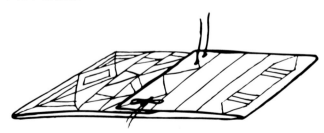

PARFLECHE DESIGNS

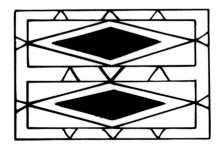

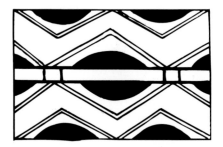

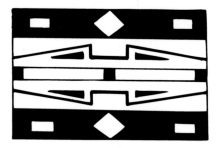

SHIELDS

THE SHIELD WAS ONE OF THE MOST VALUABLE POSSESSIONS OF THE PLAINS INDIAN. IT OFFERED MORE THAN JUST PROTECTION AGAINST ARROWS AND BULLETS; IT SAFEGUARDED AGAINST ALL FORMS OF HARM. THE SHIELD WAS MADE TO LOOK AS FIERCE AS POSSIBLE, TO STRIKE FEAR IN THE EYES OF ENEMIES. THE SYMBOLS ADORNING SHIELDS WERE BELIEVED TO CONTAIN MAGICAL POWERS TO PROTECT THE BEARER. THIS POWER, RATHER THAN THE SHIELDS THEMSELVES, WAS THE REAL MEANS OF PROTECTION.

SHIELDS WERE MADE OF THICK, HEAVY RAWHIDE TO WARD OFF SPEARS OR ARROWS AND TO RICOCHET MUSKET BULLETS. THE SYMBOLS ADORNING THEM WERE PAINTED IN A SIMPLIFIED, PICTOGRAPHIC MANNER, EACH HAVING SPECIAL SIGNIFICANCE TO THE OWNER. FREQUENTLY, OBJECTS WITH SPECIAL MEANING, SUCH AS BONES, BEAR CLAWS AND FEATHERS, WERE ATTACHED TO THE SHIELDS.

BROWN BAG IDEA

MATERIALS AND TOOLS

  TWO LARGE, PLAIN BROWN PAPER BAGS

  TWO PIECES OF CARDBOARD (AT LEAST 12" X 12")

  WHITE GLUE, GLUE DISH AND GLUE BRUSH

  ONE YARD OF HEAVY STRING OR CORD

  COMPASS OR LARGE KITCHEN PAN COVER (FOR TRACING
    CIRCLE SHAPES)

  PENCIL

  SCISSORS

  PAPER PUNCH OR NAIL

  RULER

  SINK OR LARGE BOWL OF WATER

  CRAYONS

DIRECTIONS

1. PREPARE ONE BAG TO SIMULATE A LEATHER TEXTURE BY
   SOAKING IT IN WATER FOR ABOUT TEN MINUTES. THIS
   LOOSENS THE GLUED SEAMS.

2. OPEN THE BAG AND CAREFULLY SQUEEZE OUT THE EXCESS
   WATER.

3. GENTLY SPREAD OUT THE BAG ON NEWSPAPER TO DRY.
   SOAKING AND CRUSHING THE PAPER, THEN SQUEEZING OUT
   THE WATER, WILL MAKE IT MORE PLIABLE. ANY TEARS THAT
   OCCUR DURING THE PROCESS CAN BE MENDED ON THE BACK
   WITH TAPE AFTER THE BAG HAS DRIED.

4. USE A COMPASS OR CIRCLE TEMPLATE SUCH
   AS A PAN COVER TO DRAW A 10" TO 12"
   DIAMETER CIRCLE ON THE CARDBOARD. CUT
   OUT THE CIRCLE.

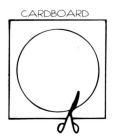

CARDBOARD

5. PLACE THE CARDBOARD CIRCLE ON THE DRY PAPER AND TRACE AROUND IT WITH A PENCIL.

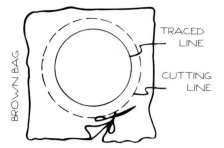

6. CAREFULLY CUT AROUND THE PAPER CIRCLE, LEAVING A 1" TO 1½" BORDER AROUND THE TRACED LINE.

7. USE THE CARDBOARD CIRCLE TO TRACE AN ADDITIONAL SHAPE ON THE SECOND, UNPREPARED PAPER BAG. USE SCISSORS TO CUT OUT A CIRCLE ½" SMALLER THAN THE TRACED CIRCULAR SHAPE. SET THIS PAPER CIRCLE ASIDE.

8. WITHIN THE BOUNDARIES OF THE FIRST TRACED CIRCLE, DRAW YOUR DESIGN AND SYMBOLS. PERHAPS YOU CAN DESIGN SYMBOLS TO TELL OF AN EXCITING ADVENTURE OR TRIP, OR TO REPRESENT AN IMAGE OF IMPORTANCE TO YOU. SOME SYMBOLS USED BY NATIVE AMERICAN TRIBES TO TELL STORIES APPEAR ON PAGE 113. PERHAPS THEY WILL SUGGEST DIFFERENT SYMBOLS THAT YOU CAN CREATE TO USE ON YOUR SHIELD. ADD COLOR TO YOUR DESIGN WITH CRAYONS.

9. POUR A SMALL AMOUNT OF GLUE (2–3 TABLESPOONS) IN THE GLUE DISH. USING THE GLUE BRUSH, COVER ONE SIDE OF THE CARDBOARD CIRCLE WITH GLUE AND PLACE IT IN THE MIDDLE OF THE BACK, UNDECORATED SIDE OF THE PAPER CIRCLE.

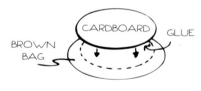

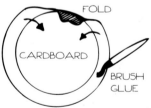

10. BRUSH GLUE ON THE BACK OF THE PAPER CIRCLE BORDER AND FOLD THE EDGES OVER THE BACK OF THE CARDBOARD CIRCLE.

LEATHERIZED
BROWN BAG

SECOND
BROWN BAG
CIRCLE

11. GLUE THE SECOND CIRCLE
WHICH YOU PREPARED EARLIER
TO THE BACK OF THE SHIELD,
COVERING THE EXPOSED
AREAS AND OVERLAPPING THE
COVERED EDGES OF THE
CARDBOARD CIRCLE.

12. PUNCH FOUR HOLES IN THE SHIELD
(TWO POSITIONED STRAIGHT ACROSS
FROM THE OTHER TWO), APPROX-
IMATELY 1" FROM THE EDGE OF THE
SHIELD.

13. THREAD HEAVY STRING OR CORD THROUGH THE HOLES SO
THAT IT CROSSES AND TIES ON THE BACK OF THE SHIELD.

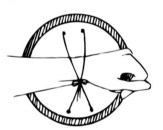

SHIELD DESIGNS

RAWHIDE VESTS

AROUND 1850, NATIVE AMERICAN TRIBES LIVING IN THE PLAINS AREA OF THE SOUTHWEST MADE THEIR CLOTHING FROM RAWHIDE. THE RAWHIDE WAS OBTAINED FROM THE BISON, AN ANIMAL RELATED TO THE NORTH AMERICAN BUFFALO. BISON ARE LARGE ANIMALS, AS TALL AS FIVE TO SIX FEET HIGH AT THE SHOULDERS. ONCE LIVING IN GREAT NUMBERS ON THE PLAINS, THE BISON IS NOW MOSTLY CONFINED TO NATIONAL PARKS. THE BISON PROVIDED FOR ALL THE HUNTER'S NEEDS: MEAT FOR FOOD, BONES FOR TOOLS AND HIDES FOR SHELTER AND CLOTHING. THEIR HIDES WERE ELABORATELY DECORATED WITH BEADS, PAINT, PORCUPINE QUILLS AND FEATHERS. SEVERAL DIFFERENT TRIBES LIVED IN THE PLAINS AREA, AND EACH DECORATED ITS LEATHER GOODS WITH DISTINCT DESIGNS AND TECHNIQUES.

BEADED VESTS ARE A COMPARATIVELY MODERN FORM OF NATIVE AMERICAN CRAFT. SOME BELIEVE THEY WERE COPIED AFTER TRADITIONAL EUROPEAN VESTS. WOODLAND INDIAN

VESTS WERE MADE OF BLACK, MAROON OR DARK BLUE VELVET AND WERE HEAVILY BEADED WITH FLORAL DESIGNS. THE PLAINS INDIAN RAWHIDE VESTS WERE LESS HEAVILY BEADED THAN THOSE OF THE WOODLAND TRIBES. DESIGNS WERE EITHER GEOMETRIC OR REALISTIC. VESTS MADE FOR MEN USUALLY DEPICTED REALISTIC DESIGNS, PICTURING SOMETHING NATURAL LIKE AN ANIMAL, WHILE GEOMETRIC PATTERNS WERE USED ON WOMEN'S VESTS.

BROWN BAG IDEA

MATERIALS AND TOOLS

- LARGE, PLAIN BROWN PAPER BAG
- BROWN TEMPERA PAINT
- CRAYONS OR FELT-TIPPED MARKERS
- SCRAP PIECES OF YARN
- BEADS, GLASS, PLASTIC OR TINTED DITALINI (PASTA DYED WITH WATER-BASED PAINT)
- LARGE DISH OF WATER
- FEATHERS (FROM FEATHER DUSTERS, CHICKEN FEATHERS OR SIMULATED WITH CONSTRUCTION PAPER)
- GLUE
- SCISSORS
- RULER
- PAPER PUNCH, AWL OR NAIL
- SINK OR LARGE BOWL OF WATER

DIRECTIONS

1. FILL A LARGE DISH ½ FULL OF WATER.

2. ADD ½ TO 1 CUP OF BROWN TEMPERA PAINT TO THE WATER.

3. PLACE THE PAPER BAG IN A SINK OR LARGE BOWL FILLED WITH CLEAR, WARM WATER, AND SOAK IT FOR A FEW MINUTES, UNTIL YOU CAN CRUMPLE IT WITHOUT UNGLUING THE SEAMS. THEN TRANSFER THE BAG TO THE DISH WITH THE WATER AND TEMPERA PAINT MIXTURE.

4. SOAK THE BAG AGAIN FOR A FEW MINUTES, THEN CAREFULLY SQUEEZE OUT THE EXCESS LIQUID. GENTLY

PLACE IT ON NEWSPAPER TO DRY. ANY TEARS THAT OCCUR
DURING THE PROCESS CAN BE MENDED ON THE INSIDE OF THE
BAG WITH TAPE AFTER THE PAPER HAS DRIED.

5. CUT A HALF CIRCLE FROM THE BOTTOM OF THE DRIED BAG
   EXTENDING ABOUT 1" FROM THE BACK OF THE BAG AND 2"
   FROM EITHER SIDE. CUT THE FRONT OF THE BAG IN HALF
   LENGTHWISE.

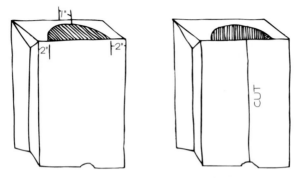

6. MEASURE DOWN 4" FROM THE BOTTOM OF THE BAG ON
   EACH SIDE OF THE CENTER CUT. CUT AT AN ANGLE FROM
   THE EDGES OF THE HALF CIRCLE ON THE BOTTOM OF THE
   BAG TO THE 4" MARKS. THIS WILL CREATE AN OPEN
   V-SHAPED NECKLINE.

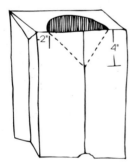
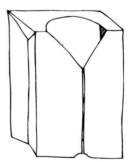

7. CUT ARMHOLES APPROXIMATELY 4"
   IN DIAMETER IN THE SIDES OF THE
   BAG, STARTING ABOUT 1" FROM THE
   BOTTOM OF THE BAG.

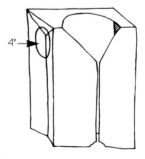

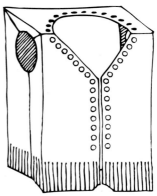

8. FOR FRINGE, MEASURE ½" INTERVALS AT THE OPEN END OF THE BAG AND CUT UP FROM THOSE MARKS APPROXIMATELY 2". PUNCH HOLES ALONG THE EDGE OF THE OPENING IN THE BOTTOM OF THE BAG AND DOWN BOTH SIDES OF THE FRONT.

9. DRAW DESIGNS ON THE VEST WITH CRAYONS OR FELT-TIPPED MARKERS. USE DESIGNS YOU WOULD LIKE TO WEAR. THESE MAY BE ORIGINAL, CONSISTING OF SHAPES AND OBJECTS OF INTEREST TO YOU, OR YOU MAY CHOOSE TRADITIONAL NATIVE AMERICAN DESIGNS OF BIRDS, HORSES, FLOWERS OR SIMPLE GEOMETRIC SHAPES.

10. THREAD YARN THROUGH THE HOLES AROUND THE VEST'S NECKLINE. ADD FEATHERS OR BEADS FOR DECORATION. FOR EXAMPLE, STRING BEADS ON YARN, THEN GLUE FEATHERS TO THE END OF THE YARN.

11. PUNCH HOLES THROUGH THE VEST WHERE YOU WOULD LIKE THE DECORATED YARN TO HANG, THEN THREAD THE YARN THROUGH THE HOLES AND SECURE IT WITH A KNOT ON THE INSIDE OF THE VEST

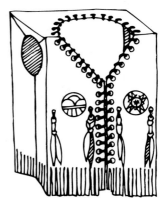

KACHINAS

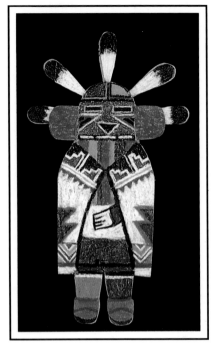

THE KACHINA IS MORE THAN A NATIVE AMERICAN DOLL. TO THE HOPI, ZUNI AND OTHER PUEBLO INDIANS, KACHINAS SYMBOLIZE ANCESTRAL SPIRITS OR DIVINE BEINGS THAT ACT AS INTERMEDIARIES BETWEEN HUMANS AND GOD. AT FESTIVAL DANCES, INDIVIDUALS IMPERSONATE KACHINAS BY WEARING MASKS AND COSTUMES REPRESENTING THESE ANCESTRAL SPIRITS. SMALL DOLLS ARE CARVED IN THE LIKENESS OF VARIOUS KACHINA DEITIES AND DISTRIBUTED TO CHILDREN BY THE MASKED DANCERS AT THESE FESTIVAL CEREMONIES. THE DOLLS ARE GIVEN TO CHILDREN AS A BLESSING, AND TO HELP THEM LEARN ABOUT THE DIFFERENT KACHINAS.

THERE ARE MORE THAN 200 DIFFERENT TYPES OF KACHINA DOLLS REPRESENTING THE DIFFERENT ANCESTRAL SPIRITS SACRED TO EACH TRIBE. THE ZUNI PRODUCE FEWER DOLLS THAN THE HOPI. ZUNI KACHINAS ARE USUALLY CARVED WITH

MOVEABLE ARMS AND LEGS WITH TINY FEET, AND ARE DRESSED IN CLOTHING. THEIR DOLLS ARE TALLER AND USUALLY THINNER THAN THOSE OF THE HOPI.

IN THE SPRING OF THE YEAR, THE PUEBLO INDIANS OF NORTHERN NEW MEXICO AND ARIZONA HOLD THEIR KACHINA FESTIVALS. IT IS BELIEVED THAT KACHINA SPIRITS HELP THE CROPS GROW AND BESTOW THEIR BLESSINGS ON THE PEOPLE, PLANTS AND ANIMALS. THE FESTIVALS CELEBRATE THIS ASPECT OF THE KACHINAS. MEN DRESS IN HUGE PAINTED MASKS AND BRIGHTLY COLORED COSTUMES TO SYMBOLIZE KACHINA SPIRITS. THEY REPRESENT BIRDS, ANIMALS, INSECTS, PLANTS, OBJECTS AND PEOPLE. EACH KACHINA HAS A NAME. SOME ACT AS CLOWNS AND ENTERTAIN THE SPECTATORS WITH MANY DIFFERENT ITEMS SUCH AS RATTLES, BOWS AND ARROWS, AND PLANTS. THESE KACHINAS ARE PAINTED BRIGHT COLORS AND DECORATED WITH FEATHERS, PELTS, HORNS, HEADDRESSES, AND ARTIFICIAL PROTRUDING EYES, EARS AND NOSES. THEY BRING GIFTS OF BOWS AND ARROWS TO THE BOYS AND SMALL KACHINA DOLLS TO THE GIRLS.

TODAY, LIKE MANY CHERISHED CRAFTS IN OTHER CULTURES, SOME KACHINAS ARE BEING MANUFACTURED COMMERCIALLY. SOME, HOWEVER, ARE STILL CARVED WITH GREAT SKILL AND BEAUTY BY NATIVE AMERICAN CRAFTSPEOPLE. THESE ARE USUALLY MADE FROM THE DRIED ROOTS OF THE COTTON-WOOD TREE. THEY ARE TYPICALLY THREE TO FOUR INCHES IN DIAMETER, VARYING IN HEIGHT. USING SAWS AND CHISELS, THE ROOTS ARE WHITTLED INTO A ROUNDED SHAPE, SMOOTHED DOWN WITH A WOOD RASP AND SANDED WITH SANDSTONE. THE HEAD, NECK, BODY AND LEGS ARE THEN CARVED. SPECIAL FEATURES SUCH AS HORNS, EARS AND PROTRUDING NOSES ARE FASHIONED OUT OF SEPARATE PIECES OF WOOD AND ATTACHED TO THE BODY. THE DOLL IS PAINTED WITH A COATING OF CLAY TO SEAL THE PORES OF THE WOOD. COMMERCIAL PRODUCTS SUCH AS GESSO ARE ALSO USED FOR THIS PURPOSE. ORIGINALLY, NATURAL SOURCES WERE USED FOR PIGMENTS, LIKE COPPER CARBONATE FOR GREEN, SOOT FOR BLACK AND GROUND HEMATITE FOR RED. NOW WATER-BASED PAINTS ARE USED BY MANY KACHINA ARTISTS. THE COLORS USED FOR KACHINAS ARE OFTEN SYMBOLIC. THE HOPI RECOGNIZE SIX BASIC DIRECTIONS, EACH ASSOCIATED WITH

A COLOR. NORTH IS INDICATED BY YELLOW, WEST BY BLUE-GREEN, SOUTH BY RED AND EAST, WHITE. ALL THINGS ABOVE ARE REPRESENTED BY GRAY AND ALL THINGS DIRECTLY BELOW BY BLACK.

BROWN BAG IDEA

MATERIALS AND TOOLS

LARGE, PLAIN BROWN PAPER BAG

PENCIL

CRAYONS, FELT-TIPPED MARKERS OR WATER-BASED PAINT

RULER

SCISSORS

WHITE GLUE

NEWSPAPER (FOR STUFFING)

FEATHERS FROM A FEATHER DUSTER OR OBTAINED FROM A CHICKEN FARM, YARN, SHELLS OR CLOTH (ALL OPTIONAL)

DIRECTIONS

1. CUT THE PAPER BAG APART AT THE BACK SEAM, AND CUT OFF THE BOTTOM SECTION.

2. FOLD THE BAG IN HALF HORIZONTALLY AND CUT ALONG THE FOLD.

3. WITH A PENCIL, DRAW THE OUTLINE OF YOUR KACHINA FIGURE ON ONE PIECE OF THE BAG. YOU MAY CHOOSE TO MAKE A DOLL PORTRAYING THE SPIRIT OF THE NATIVE AMERICAN KACHINAS OR REPRESENTING CHARACTERISTICS THAT HAVE SPECIAL SIGNIFICANCE TO YOU.

4. WITH CRAYONS, PAINT OR FELT-TIPPED MARKERS, COLOR IN A DESIGN ON YOUR OUTLINED KACHINA. USE A RULER FOR STRAIGHT LINES, IF NECESSARY.

5. CAREFULLY CUT OUT THE KACHINA.

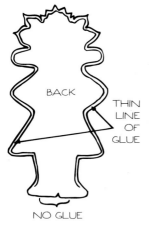

BACK

THIN
LINE
OF
GLUE

NO GLUE

6. TURN OVER THE KACHINA, COLORED SIDE DOWN. CAREFULLY RUN A THIN LINE OF GLUE ALL AROUND THE EDGE, EXCEPT ACROSS THE BOTTOM EDGE, WHERE STUFFING WILL BE INSERTED.

7. PLACE THE FIGURE, GLUE SIDE DOWN, ON THE OTHER HALF OF THE BROWN PAPER BAG.

8. ALLOW THE GLUE TO DRY, AND CUT OUT THE KACHINA FIGURE.

9. BEGIN COLORING THE BACK OF THE KACHINA. BE SURE TO CONSIDER THE RELATIONSHIP OF THE BACK DESIGN TO THE FRONT DESIGN.

10. CRUSH SMALL PIECES OF NEWSPAPER AND CAREFULLY STUFF THE KACHINA.

11. SEAL THE KACHINA'S BOTTOM EDGE WITH GLUE.

12. IF DESIRED, ADD FEATHERS OR OTHER DECORATIVE MATERIALS.

SCROLLS

MANY NATIVE AMERICAN TRIBES INVENTED WAYS TO
RECORD FACTS AND IDEAS WITH GRAPHIC SYMBOLS. OBJECTS
WERE DRAWN AS THE PEOPLE EXPERIENCED THEM, NOT AS
THEY APPEARED TO THE EYE. MOUNTAINS WERE PICTURED AS
TRIANGLES, TRAILS DESIGNATED BY BROKEN LINES. DEAD
ANIMALS WERE PICTURED LYING ON THEIR BACKS WITH THEIR
FEET AND LEGS UP. ONE ARROW SPELLED PEACE, TWO
ARROWS PASSING IN OPPOSITE DIRECTIONS SIGNALED WAR. THE
SIGNS WERE UNDERSTOOD ON SIGHT BY MEMBERS OF THE SAME
TRIBE OR GROUPS OF TRIBES TO HAVE THE SAME MEANING. NOT
EVERY DESIGN PAINTED ON A LEATHER SCROLL OR ROBE
REPRESENTED A HIDDEN MEANING. SOME WERE PAINTED THE
WAY THE NATIVE AMERICAN ARTIST HAD PERSONALLY SEEN
OR FELT THEM OR FOR DECORATION.

BROWN BAG IDEA

MATERIALS AND TOOLS

ONE OR TWO LARGE, PLAIN BROWN PAPER BAGS

CRAYONS OR FELT-TIPPED MARKERS

TWO STRAIGHT STICKS OR DOWL RODS, APPROXIMATELY
12" LONG

PLAIN DRAWING PAPER

GLUE

SINK OR LARGE BOWL OF WATER

DIRECTIONS

1. PREPARE BAG TO SIMULATE LEATHER BY SOAKING IT IN
   WATER FOR ABOUT TEN MINUTES. THIS LOOSENS THE GLUED
   SEAMS.

2. OPEN THE BAG CAREFULLY AND SQUEEZE OUT THE EXCESS
   WATER.

3. GENTLY SPREAD OUT THE BAG ON NEWSPAPER TO DRY.
   SOAKING AND CRUSHING THE PAPER, THEN SQUEEZING OUT
   THE WATER, WILL MAKE IT MORE PLIABLE. ANY TEARS THAT
   OCCUR DURING THE PROCESS CAN BE MENDED ON THE BACK
   WITH TAPE AFTER THE PAPER HAS DRIED.

4. PLAN A STORY TO TELL USING GRAPHIC SYMBOLS. YOU MAY
   USE THE NATIVE AMERICAN SYMBOLS PROVIDED IN THE
   CHART OR DESIGN SYMBOLS THAT HAVE MORE DIRECT
   MEANING TO YOU. IF YOU CHOOSE TO DESIGN YOUR OWN,
   BEGIN BY CONSIDERING SYMBOLS THAT YOU ARE ALREADY
   FAMILIAR WITH, SUCH AS TRAFFIC, SAFETY OR WARNING
   SYMBOLS. YOU MIGHT DESIGN A SCROLL ILLUSTRATING THE
   ROUTE FROM YOUR HOME TO A FAMILIAR PLACE, SUCH AS
   YOUR SCHOOL, GROCERY STORE OR FRIEND'S HOUSE. WHAT
   WOULD BE SOME OF THE LANDMARKS OR OBJECTS ALONG
   THE ROUTE?

   YOU MIGHT PASS A HOUSE WITH A BARKING

   TURN LEFT AT THE CORNER BY THE FIRST

   THEN WALK THREE

5. DECIDE THE SYMBOLS YOU NEED TO DESIGN AND MAKE A CHART OF THEM.

6. DETERMINE THE SIZE AND LENGTH OF PAPER NEEDED TO TELL YOUR STORY. TWO BAGS MAY BE GLUED TOGETHER TO TELL A LONG TALE. CUT THE PAPER'S WIDTH TO FIT YOUR END STICKS, ALLOWING FOR AT LEAST A 1" OVERHANG OF STICK ON BOTH THE TOP AND BOTTOM EDGES OF THE PAPER. THESE OVERHANGING STICK ENDS WILL SERVE AS HANDLES. ALLOW ABOUT 3" OF MARGIN AT EITHER END OF YOUR PAPER FOR GLUING THE STICKS IN PLACE.

7. PLAN THE LAYOUT OF YOUR STORY ON A SHEET OF PLAIN DRAWING PAPER, THEN DRAW IT ON THE BROWN PAPER WITH CRAYONS OR FELT-TIPPED MARKERS.

8. PUT GLUE ON THE 3" MARGIN AT EACH END OF THE SCROLL. PLACE THE STICKS ON TOP OF THE GLUE AND ROLL THE PAPER OVER THE STICKS, SECURING THE STICKS IN PLACE.

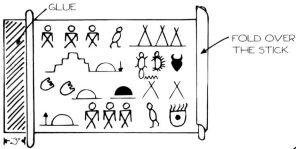

9. ROLL THE STICKS INWARD TOWARDS THE CENTER OF THE SCROLL AND LET THE GLUE DRY.

NATIVE AMERICAN SYMBOLS

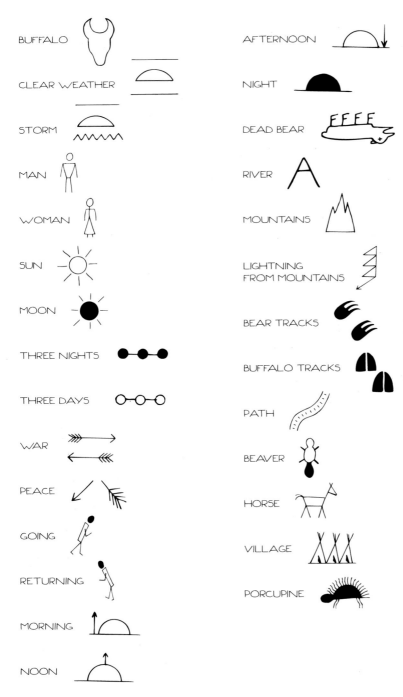

BUFFALO

CLEAR WEATHER

STORM

MAN

WOMAN

SUN

MOON

THREE NIGHTS

THREE DAYS

WAR

PEACE

GOING

RETURNING

MORNING

NOON

AFTERNOON

NIGHT

DEAD BEAR

RIVER

MOUNTAINS

LIGHTNING FROM MOUNTAINS

BEAR TRACKS

BUFFALO TRACKS

PATH

BEAVER

HORSE

VILLAGE

PORCUPINE

THUNDERBIRD RUGS

THE NAVAJO LEARNED THE ART OF WEAVING FROM THE
PUEBLO INDIANS. AT FIRST, THE PATTERNS THEY WOVE WERE
SIMPLE: PRIMARILY NARROW STRIPES AND BANDS. COLORS WERE
NATURAL WOOL TONES OF WHITE, GRAY, BROWN, TAN AND
BLACK. OVER TIME, THE NAVAJO BECAME QUITE SKILLED AT
CREATING WOVEN BLANKETS. BY 1850, THEY WERE SUPPLYING
BLANKETS TO THE SETTLERS, TRADERS AND THE U.S. MILITARY.
THE TRADERS BROUGHT MACHINE-MADE YARN IN BRIGHT
COLORS TO THE WEAVERS, AND BLANKET PATTERNS WERE
INFUSED WITH BOLD AND BRILLIANT COLOR.

AS THE TWENTIETH CENTURY APPROACHED, REGIONAL
STYLES OF WEAVING BEGAN TO DEVELOP. WEAVERS STOPPED
MAKING BLANKETS FOR THEIR OWN USE, AND BEGAN TO
WEAVE RUGS FOR THE TOURIST MARKET. BECAUSE OF THEIR
SIMILARITIES, IT IS OFTEN DIFFICULT TO DISTINGUISH BLANKETS
OF THE 1890S FROM RUGS OF THE SAME PERIOD. AT THIS TIME,
A NEW COMMERCIAL YARN CALLED GERMANTOWN WAS

INTRODUCED AS A TRADE ITEM. THE WEAVERS WORKED WITH THE GREAT RANGE OF GERMANTOWN COLORS TO CREATE A WIDE VARIETY OF NEW PATTERNS. SOME OF THESE PATTERNED RUGS CONTAINED SQUARES WITH INDIVIDUAL DESIGN MOTIFS.

ANOTHER REGIONAL STYLE OF WEAVING WAS THE PICTORIAL. PICTORIALS DEMONSTRATED A VARIETY OF DESIGN STYLES AND SUBJECT MATTER, SUCH AS ANIMALS, PATRIOTIC SYMBOLS AND POPULAR AMERICAN ICONS (I.E., SUPERMAN, MICKEY MOUSE). STYLIZED FIGURES FLOATED IN SOLID COLOR BACKGROUNDS.

TODAY, WEAVINGS ARE OFTEN DONE TO HANG ON WALLS. PERHAPS THIS IS BECAUSE COLLECTORS OF BOTH MODERN AND PERIOD WEAVINGS ARE RELUCTANT TO WALK ON THEIR RUGS.

DECORATIVE MOTIFS THAT MIGHT BE USED ON NATIVE AMERICAN RUGS INCLUDE THE THUNDERBIRD AND THE ROSETTE. BOTH ARE GEOMETRIC IN DESIGN.

THE THUNDERBIRD WAS REVERED BY PRACTICALLY ALL NATIVE AMERICAN TRIBES. SOME CONSIDERED IT TO BE A DEITY, A CREATURE OF ENORMOUS SIZE CAPABLE OF PRODUCING THUNDER BY FLAPPING ITS WINGS AND LIGHTNING BY OPENING AND CLOSING ITS EYES. EACH TRIBE DEPICTED THE THUNDERBIRD DIFFERENTLY.

ROSETTE MOTIFS ARE ORNAMENTS THAT ARE OFTEN PUT ON HEADBANDS (AS PART OF DANCE COSTUMES), BISON ROBES, SHIRTS AND TEPEES. THEY ARE TRADITIONALLY WORN IN THE MIDDLE OF THE FOREHEAD AS BRILLIANT CIRCLES OF COLOR. THERE ARE MANY TYPES OF ROSETTES, BUT THE MOST COMMON CONSIST OF A CENTER SURROUNDED BY BRILLIANTLY COLORED FEATHERS OR HAIR. THE CENTERS ARE MADE OF BEADS, MIRRORS, HARNESS STUDS OR PIECES OF FELT. ROSETTES RANGE FROM FOUR TO SIX INCHES IN DIAMETER. BEADED ROSETTE CENTER DESIGNS CONSIST OF CONCENTRIC CIRCLES AND STAR SHAPES.

THUNDERBIRD AND ROSETTE DESIGNS

BROWN BAG IDEA

MATERIALS and TOOLS

    ONE OR TWO LARGE, PLAIN BROWN PAPER BAGS
        (THE SIZE OF YOUR RUG WILL DETERMINE THE NUMBER
        OF BAGS USED.)

    SINK OR LARGE BOWL OF WATER

    BROWN TEMPERA PAINT

    SCISSORS

    CONSTRUCTION PAPER

    PAPER PUNCH, AWL OR NAIL

    FELT-TIPPED MARKERS OR CRAYONS

    YARN

    NEEDLE (DARNING TYPE, WITH LARGE EYE)

    IRON

DIRECTIONS

1. DECIDE THE SIZE AND PROPORTIONS OF YOUR RUG, AND NUMBER OF DESIGNS YOU WOULD LIKE TO INCLUDE. SIX TO TWELVE MOTIFS WILL GIVE YOU A NICE SELECTION OF PATCHES. A LARGE RUG MAY REQUIRE USING MORE THAN ONE BROWN PAPER BAG.

2. FILL THE SINK OR A LARGE BOWL ½ FULL OF WARM WATER. ADD ½ CUP OF BROWN TEMPERA PAINT.

3. CRUMPLE THE PAPER BAG OR BAGS CAREFULLY. GIVE THE BAG(S) A CLOTH-LIKE TEXTURE BY SOAKING IN THE WATER AND PAINT MIXTURE FOR ABOUT TEN MINUTES. THIS LOOSENS THE GLUED SEAMS.

4. OPEN THE BAG(S) AND CAREFULLY SQUEEZE OUT THE EXCESS WATER. GENTLY SPREAD THE BAG(S) OUT ON NEWSPAPER TO DRY. SOAKING AND CRUSHING THE PAPER, THEN SQUEEZING OUT THE WATER, WILL MAKE IT MORE PLIABLE. ANY TEARS THAT OCCUR CAN BE MENDED ON THE BACK WITH TAPE AFTER THE PAPER HAS DRIED.

5. WITH A WARM IRON, PRESS THE DRIED PAPER BAG(S). GLUE OR TAPE THE TWO BAGS TOGETHER, IF WORKING ON A LARGE RUG.

6. CUT THE PAPER TO THE APPROPRIATE SIZE AND SHAPE FOR YOUR RUG, AS DETERMINED IN STEP 1. DECIDE THE LENGTH OF FRINGE YOU WOULD LIKE FOR YOUR RUG. MEASURE BOTH ENDS OF THE PAPER ACCORDINGLY.

7. CAREFULLY CUT FRINGES ¼" TO ½" WIDE.

8. SELECT COLORS FOR PATCHES TO DECORATE YOUR RUG. CUT SQUARES OF CONSTRUCTION PAPER IN THE COLORS OF YOUR CHOICE. A 3" TO 4" SQUARE IS A GOOD SIZE FOR A PATCH.

9. USE FELT-TIPPED MARKERS OR CRAYONS TO DESIGN THE PATCHES. EACH COLOR PATCH SHOULD HAVE ONE DESIGN ON IT. REFER TO THE CHART OF THUNDERBIRD AND ROSETTE DESIGNS FOR EXAMPLES OF TRADITIONAL NATIVE AMERICAN MOTIFS. ARRANGE THE PATCHES ON THE BROWN PAPER RUG.

10. WITH THE PAPER PUNCH, AWL OR NAIL, PUNCH HOLES IN THE CORNER OF EACH PATCH, ½" IN AND ½" DOWN FROM EACH CORNER.

11. USE THE YARN AND NEEDLE TO ATTACH THE PATCHES TO THE BACKGROUND BROWN PAPER RUG BY SEWING THROUGH THE HOLES IN EACH PATCH AND PUNCTURING CORRESPONDING HOLES IN THE BROWN PAPER RUG.

BONE BREASTPLATES

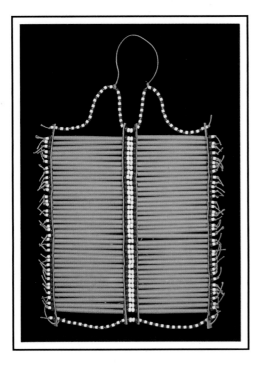

DISTINCTIVE BONE AND BUCKSKIN BREASTPLATES WERE WORN BY THE NATIVE AMERICANS OF THE WESTERN PLAINS. THE BREASTPLATES DATING FROM THE LATE 1800S WERE CONSIDERED STATUS SYMBOLS. THEY WERE MADE FROM LONG, SLENDER COW BONES, CALLED HAIR PIPES. THE BONES ARE ABOUT ¼" THICK AT THE MIDDLE, TAPER TOWARD THE ENDS AND MAY VARY FROM 3 ½" TO 5 ½" IN LENGTH. THESE BONES WERE USED AS A MEDIUM OF EXCHANGE IN TRADING AND BREASTPLATES MADE FROM THE BONES WERE VALUED ACCORDING TO THE NUMBER OF BONES INCLUDED, THEIR LENGTH AND THEIR QUALITY. WHILE BREASTPLATES WERE MADE MAINLY FOR MEN, COLLARS CONSTRUCTED IN A SIMILAR FASHION WERE MADE FOR WOMEN. THOSE CREATED FOR MEN CAME TO THE WAIST OR JUST BELOW IT. WOMEN'S COLLARS RANGED IN LENGTH, FROM WAIST LEVEL TO JUST ABOVE THE GROUND. BOTH COMBINED HAIR PIPES WITH GLASS BEADS AND WERE STRUNG WITH LEATHER STRIPS THAT SEPARATED AND HELD THE STRANDS TOGETHER.

Once considered a type of armor, the breastplate became a popular chest ornament for its fashion, status and trade value. The breastplate is still one of the most important pieces of tribal dance regalia worn at Native American celebrations throughout the country.

BROWN BAG IDEA

MATERIALS and TOOLS

   3 LARGE, PLAIN BROWN PAPER BAGS (TWO FOR BEADS
      AND ANOTHER FOR STRAPS)

   PENCIL

   RULER

   SCISSORS

   GLUE

   PAPER PUNCH

   APPROXIMATELY 200 BEADS MADE OF GLASS, PLASTIC OR
      TINTED DITALINI (PASTA DYED WITH WATER-BASED
      PAINT)

   BROWN SISAL OR JUTE WRAPPING TWINE

DIRECTIONS for MAKING HAIR PIPE BEADS

1. CUT ONE OF THE PAPER BAGS APART AT THE BACK SEAM, AND CUT OFF THE BOTTOM SECTION.

2. FOLD THE BAG IN HALF LENGTHWISE. CUT THE BAG AT THE FOLD. YOU SHOULD HAVE TWO STRIPS APPROXIMATELY 30–40" LONG AND 8 ½" WIDE.

3. START AT THE TOP LEFT CORNER OF ONE OF THE PIECES OF PAPER, AND USE YOUR RULER TO DIVIDE IT INTO 5" SECTIONS.

4. STARTING AT THE BOTTOM LEFT CORNER OF THE STRIP, MEASURE OVER 2 ½". FROM THE 2 ½" MARK, DIVIDE THE BOTTOM EDGE INTO 5" SECTIONS.

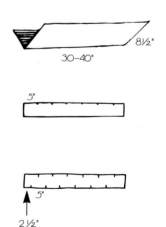

5. DRAW LINES CONNECTING THE TOP AND BOTTOM DIVISION MARKS AS SHOWN.

6. REPEAT STEPS 2 THROUGH 5 WITH THE OTHER STRIP FROM THE BAG, THEN REPEAT THE ENTIRE PROCESS WITH A SECOND BROWN PAPER BAG.

7. CAREFULLY CUT ALONG THE PENCILED LINES. EACH BAG SHOULD YIELD APPROXI-MATELY 25 PAPER BEADS. YOU WILL NEED APPROXIMATELY 50 FOR THE BREASTPLATE. YOU MAY USE AN EXTRA BROWN BAG TO STORE YOUR BEADS IN UNTIL YOU ARE READY TO STRING THEM.

8. STARTING AT THE WIDE END OF EACH PAPER TRIANGLE, ROLL IT AROUND A PENCIL UNTIL YOU REACH THE POINT OF THE TRIANGLE.

9. PUT A BIT OF GLUE ON THE POINT AND SEAL IT TO THE BEAD, THEN REMOVE THE PENCIL. REPEAT THE PROCESS FOR EACH TRIANGLE.

DIRECTIONS for MAKING the STRAPS

1. CUT APART THE THIRD PAPER BAG, FOLLOWING THE PROCEDURE IN STEP 1 FOR MAKING THE BEADS.

2. FROM THE OPENED BAG, CUT FOUR STRIPS 3" WIDE AND 14" LONG.

3. FOLD EACH STRIP IN HALF ONCE LENGTHWISE, THEN FOLD IN HALF LENGTHWISE AGAIN SO THAT YOU HAVE FOUR THICKNESSES OF PAPER. EACH OF THE FOUR LENGTHS OF PAPER WILL FORM A STRAP FOR YOUR BREASTPLATE.

4. WITH A ⅛" PAPER PUNCH, PUT HOLES EVERY ½" DOWN THE ENTIRE LENGTH OF EACH STRAP, THROUGH THE CENTER OF THE FOLDED STRAP.

DIRECTIONS for STRINGING the BEADS

1. CUT THE SISAL OR JUTE TWINE INTO 25 PIECES, EACH 15" LONG.

2. TIE A KNOT AT THE END OF ONE PIECE OF TWINE.

3. BEGIN BY STRINGING TWO NON-PAPER BEADS (GLASS, PLASTIC, DITALINI), THEN FEED THE TWINE THROUGH THE SECOND HOLE DOWN IN ONE OF THE STRAPS. STRING ONE HAIR PIPE BEAD ON THE TWINE AND FEED THE TWINE THROUGH THE SECOND HOLE DOWN IN A SECOND PAPER STRAP. STRING AT LEAST FOUR NON-PAPER BEADS AND FEED THE TWINE THROUGH THE SECOND HOLE DOWN IN A THIRD PAPER STRAP. STRING A HAIR PIPE BEAD, FEED THE TWINE THROUGH THE SECOND HOLE DOWN IN THE LAST STRAP AND FINISH BY STRINGING TWO ENDING BEADS.

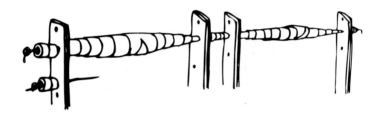

4. PULL THE TWINE FIRMLY BUT NOT TOO TIGHT, AND SECURE THE OTHER END WITH A KNOT.

5. REPEAT STEPS 1 THROUGH 4, STRINGING THROUGH EVERY SUBSEQUENT HOLE OF THE STRAPS UNTIL YOU HAVE COMPLETED STRINGING THE DESIRED NUMBER OF BEADS.

DIRECTIONS for MAKING the TIE STRINGS

1. MAKE A KNOT IN THE END OF A PIECE OF TWINE 20–24" LONG.

2. STRING ONE OR TWO NON-PAPER BEADS, AND THEN PUT THE STRING THROUGH THE FIRST HOLE IN ONE OF THE OUTER STRAPS.

3. STRING 25–30 NON-PAPER BEADS, THEN STRING THE TWINE THROUGH THE FIRST HOLE OF THE FIRST CENTER STRAP.

4. STRING FOUR BEADS BETWEEN THE CENTER STRAPS.

5. STRING 20–30 NON-PAPER BEADS BETWEEN THE THIRD AND FOURTH STRAPS.

6. STRING ONE OR TWO BEADS THROUGH THE END OF THE STRAP AND KNOT THE TWINE.

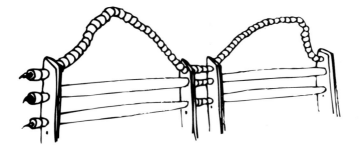

7. TIE THE TWINE AS PICTURED IN THE PHOTOGRAPH OF THE FINISHED BREASTPLATE TO GO AROUND YOUR NECK AND WAIST.

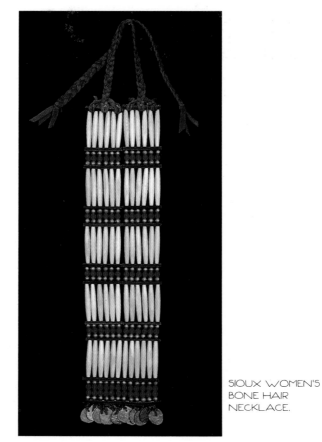

SIOUX WOMEN'S BONE HAIR NECKLACE.

PAINTED BUFFALO ROBES

PAINTING ON ANIMAL HIDES WAS ONE OF THE MOST OUTSTANDING ART FORMS OF THE PLAINS INDIANS. THE WORKS WERE CUSTOMARILY PAINTED BY MEN TO NARRATE ADVENTURES, RECORD HISTORICAL EVENTS OR INDICATE THE WEALTH OF THE HIDE'S OWNER. REPRESENTATIVE PAINTINGS OF BATTLE AND HUNTING SCENES WERE DONE EXCLUSIVELY BY THE MEN. THESE OUTSTANDING TRIBAL EVENTS WERE PORTRAYED THROUGH PICTOGRAPHS, IN WHICH A PICTURE REPRESENTS AN IDEA. THEY WERE PAINTED FROM LEFT TO RIGHT. THE HIDES WERE OFTEN SEWN INTO ROBES FOR BOTH MEN AND WOMEN. WOMEN'S ROBES WERE PAINTED WITH GEOMETRIC DESIGNS CONSISTING OF SUNBURST AND BOX-SHAPED FORMS WITH BORDERS.

DEER AND ELK WERE THE MOST IMPORTANT ANIMALS FOR FOOD AND HIDES. THE HIDES WERE USED TO MAKE CLOTHING, TEPEE COVERS, SHIELDS AND BOATS, AND CONTAINERS FOR FOOD, MEDICINES, GUNS AND EVEN BABIES. FURS BECAME AN

IMPORTANT MEANS OF EXCHANGE WITH TRADERS FOR GOODS SUCH AS KNIVES, GUNS, POTS, BEADS AND CLOTH.

FURS OF LARGE ANIMALS WERE USED FOR ROBES, WHICH WERE WORN IN BOTH WINTER AND SUMMER. THE WINTER ROBE WAS MADE FROM THE HIDE OF A BUFFALO COW AND TANNED WITH THE FUR LEFT ON. SUMMER ROBES WERE MADE OF HIDES FROM WHICH ALL THE HAIR HAD BEEN REMOVED.

HIDES REQUIRED MUCH HARD WORK TO PREPARE THEM FOR PAINTING. UNTREATED SKINS BECOME STIFF AND HARD AND BEGIN TO ROT. IN THE SOUTHWEST AND NORTHEAST, PREPARATION OF THE SKINS WAS TRADITIONALLY DONE BY MEN, BUT IN MOST OF NORTH AMERICA, PREPARATION WAS DONE MAINLY BY WOMEN. FIRST THE SKINS WERE STAKED OUT ON THE GROUND. CHISEL-LIKE TOOLS MADE FROM BUFFALO BONES WERE USED TO CHIP OFF THE FLESH. AFTER DRYING IN THE SUN, THE HIDE WAS SCRAPED TO THIN IT. IF THE HIDE WAS TO BE USED FOR RAWHIDE, THE HAIR WAS SCRAPED OFF.

PAINTS FOR HIDE DRAWING WERE MADE FROM ANIMAL, VEGETABLE AND MINERAL SOURCES. RED PAINTS WERE MADE FROM RED EARTH AND CRUSHED ROCK. YELLOW WAS MADE FROM CLAY, BLUE FROM THE DROPPINGS OF WILD DUCKS, GREEN FROM PLANTS AND BLACK FROM DIRT. PIGMENTS WERE GROUND AND MIXED WITH WATER. CHARCOAL STICKS WERE USED TO OUTLINE THE DRAWINGS. THE FINISHED PAINTINGS WERE SEALED WITH A COATING OF GLUE.

SINCE NATIVE AMERICAN TRIBES HAD NO WRITTEN LANGUAGE, THE ARTWORK OF THESE PICTOGRAPHS HAS RECORDED THE HISTORY OF THE PLAINS INDIANS FOR FUTURE GENERATIONS.

BROWN BAG IDEA

MATERIALS AND TOOLS

    LARGE, PLAIN BROWN PAPER BAG
    SINK OR LARGE BOWL OF WATER
    CRAYONS OR FELT-TIPPED MARKERS
    PENCIL
    NEWSPAPERS

DIRECTIONS

1. GIVE THE BAG A HIDE-LIKE TEXTURE BY SOAKING IT IN WATER FOR ABOUT TEN MINUTES. THIS LOOSENS THE GLUED SEAMS.

2. OPEN THE BAG AND CAREFULLY SQUEEZE OUT THE EXCESS WATER.

3. GENTLY SPREAD OUT THE BAG ON NEWSPAPER TO DRY. SOAKING AND CRUSHING THE PAPER, THEN SQUEEZING OUT THE WATER, WILL MAKE IT MORE PLIABLE. ANY TEARS THAT OCCUR DURING THE PROCESS CAN BE MENDED ON THE BACK WITH TAPE AFTER THE PAPER HAS DRIED.

4. FOLD THE PREPARED BAG IN HALF LENGTHWISE.

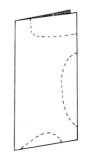

5. TEAR THE BAG AS INDICATED BY THE BROKEN LINES.

6. REFER TO THE CHART OF NATIVE AMERICAN SYMBOLS TO PLAN YOUR DESIGN. YOU MAY WANT TO USE GEOMETRIC DESIGNS ON YOUR HIDE, OR YOU MAY WANT TO USE SYMBOLS TO TELL A VISUAL STORY. OPEN THE BAG AND SKETCH IN PENCIL THE PLACEMENT OF YOUR DESIGNS.

7. COLOR THE DESIGN USING FELT-TIPPED MARKERS OR CRAYONS. PRESS CRAYONS DOWN HARD TO GET STRONG COLOR.

NATIVE AMERICAN SYMBOLS

DEAD BEAR

ATTACK ON
ENEMY VILLAGE

PEACE

WAR

BUFFALO
TRACKS

MAN

DEER

MOUNTAIN

WOMAN

TEPEE

RAIN

RAINBOW

MOUNTAINS

HORSE

HOGAN
(HOME)

PEACE PIPE

BATTLE
SCENE

SUN

MOON

RUNNING
WATER

PAINTED BUFFALO ROBE DESIGNS

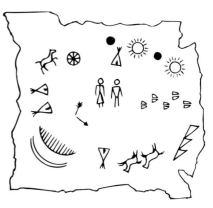

TAPA CLOTH FROM HAWAII.

POLYNESIA

ABORIGINAL BARK PAINTINGS   130

HAWAIIAN TAPA CLOTH   134

ABORIGINAL BARK PAINTINGS

ABORIGINES WERE THE FIRST AUSTRALIANS. THEY NEVER
DEVELOPED AN AGRICULTURAL SOCIETY, AND WANDERED
ACROSS THE LAND INSTEAD, FITTING THEIR NEEDS TO WHAT
THE ENVIRONMENT HAD TO OFFER. THEY WERE ARMED WITH
THE SIMPLEST WEAPONS: THE SPEAR, THE THROWING STICK
(BOOMERANG) AND THE STONE KNIFE. WHEN SETTLERS
ARRIVED FROM EUROPE IN THE LATE EIGHTEENTH CENTURY,
THE IMMIGRANTS TOOK POSSESSION OF THE LAND. DEFENSELESS
AGAINST THEIR WEAPONS, THE ABORIGINES LOST THEIR
HUNTING GROUNDS, AND MANY DIED. SOME DESCENDANTS OF
THOSE TRIBES NOW LIVE ON THE OUTSKIRTS OF AUSTRALIAN
CITIES.

ARNHEM LAND, A SECTION OF THE NORTHERN COAST OF
AUSTRALIA'S NORTHERN TERRITORY, HAS BEEN SET ASIDE AS
ONE OF THE COUNTRY'S ABORIGINAL RESERVES. ABORIGINE
DESCENDANTS LIVE IN THIS HARSH, BARREN PART OF
AUSTRALIA, PURSUING THEIR WAY OF LIFE AS THEY HAVE FOR

30,000 YEARS. THEY HAVE LITTLE CONTACT WITH WESTERN CIVILIZATION, BUT THEIR DESIGNS, PARTICULARLY THOSE PAINTED ON EUCALYPTUS BARK PANELS, ARE OF GREAT INTEREST WORLDWIDE.

ABORIGINES HAVE DEVELOPED THREE SEPARATE STYLES OF BARK PAINTING. THE MAIN STYLE, PRACTICED IN CENTRAL ARNHEM LAND, FEATURES ONE OR MORE FIGURES ON A PLAIN, DARK BACKGROUND. TO THE WEST, THE X-RAY STYLE PREDOMINATES, IN WHICH THE ARTIST PAINTS NOT ONLY THE EXTERNAL FORM OF A HUMAN BEING OR CREATURE BUT ALSO THE INTERNAL DETAILS, SUCH AS THE SKELETON, HEART, LUNGS AND OTHER ORGANS. THE MOST COMPLEX COMPOSITIONS COME FROM NORTHEAST ARNHEM LAND. HERE, DRAWINGS COVERING THE PANEL AND ITS BACKGROUND ARE FILLED AND FRAMED WITH HATCHED OR DOTTED DESIGNS. THE PLAID-LIKE HATCHING IS A "CLAN-OWNED" PATTERN, WHICH ONLY CLAN MEMBERS CAN USE.

TO PREPARE PANELS FOR PAINTING, CURVED SLABS OF STRINGY BARK ARE STRIPPED FROM THE EUCALYPTUS TREE. THESE ARE STEAMED OVER HOT COALS TO REMOVE THE OUTER FIBROUS SURFACE BEFORE THE BARK IS PLACED ON THE GROUND AND COVERED WITH SAND TO DRY FOR A FEW DAYS.

THE RED, WHITE AND YELLOW COLORS USED IN ABORIGINAL PAINTINGS ARE MADE FROM GROUND OCHRE MIXED WITH WATER. THE BLACK IS A CARBON COMPOUND, AND AN OLIVE COLOR IS THE COMBINATION OF BLACK AND YELLOW. WHITE IS OBTAINED FROM PIPE CLAY. THE JUICE OF AN ORCHID PLANT

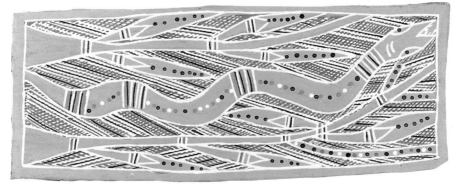

MANGROVE SNAKE, BARK PAINTING BY MANAWILA DAYGURRGURR, AUSTRALIA.

IS USED AS A FIXATIVE TO PREVENT PAINT FROM FLAKING. CHEWED TWIGS OR FRAYED LEAF EDGES MAKE PAINT BRUSHES. FINE LINES ARE MADE WITH A FEATHER OR A FEW HAIRS FASTENED TO A HANDLE.

BROWN BAG IDEA

MATERIALS AND TOOLS

LARGE, PLAIN BROWN PAPER BAG

FELT-TIPPED PENS OR CRAYONS IN BROWN, BLACK, RUST
AND YELLOW

WHITE CHALK, PENCIL OR CRAYON

SCISSORS

RULER (OPTIONAL)

DIRECTIONS

1. CUT THE PAPER BAG APART AT THE BACK SEAM AND CUT OFF THE BOTTOM SECTION.

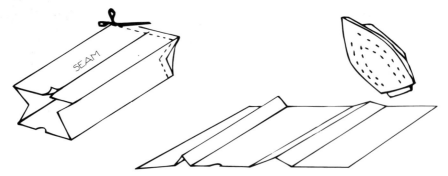

2. PRESS THE BAG WITH A WARM IRON TO FLATTEN THE CREASES.

3. CUT THE BAG TO MAKE THE SIZE PAINTING YOU WOULD LIKE.

4. WITH THE WHITE PENCIL, CHALK OR CRAYON, LIGHTLY SKETCH YOUR DESIGN ON THE BAG. YOUR FAVORITE ANIMALS MAKE GOOD SUBJECTS FOR THIS PROJECT. CAN YOU IMAGINE HOW PICTURING THEIR INTERNAL ORGANS MIGHT ADD TO YOUR DESIGNS? TRY CONNECTING THE FIGURES WITH PATTERNS OF HATCHED LINES. LIMIT YOUR-SELF TO THE EARTH COLORS RUST, YELLOW, BROWN, BLACK

AND WHITE. SOME EXAMPLES OF ABORIGINAL DESIGNS ARE
SHOWN HERE. YOU MIGHT WANT TO USE SOME OF THESE
MOTIFS TO HELP DEVELOP YOUR OWN IDEAS FOR YOUR
PROJECT.

5. DRAW YOUR FINAL DESIGN WITH THE FELT-TIPPED MARKERS
    OR CRAYONS.

ABORIGINAL DESIGNS

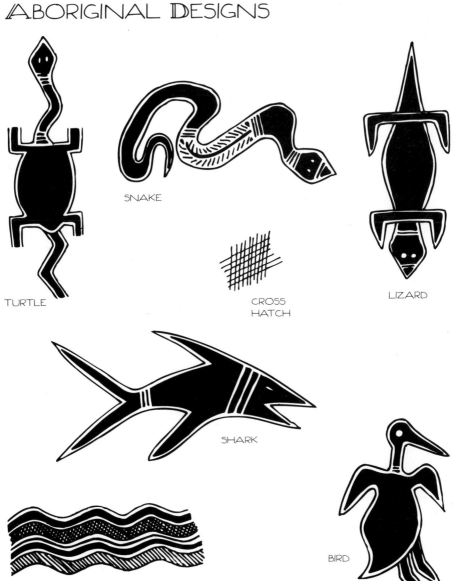

TURTLE

SNAKE

CROSS
HATCH

LIZARD

SHARK

WATER HOLE

BIRD

HAWAIIAN TAPA CLOTH

One of the most outstanding examples of Hawaiian craftsmanship is tapa, a bark cloth. Tapa cloth was the traditional fabric of Polynesia, a group of islands located in the Pacific Ocean. It was used for clothing, room dividers, floor coverings, bedding and decoration on ceremonial and royal occasions.

To make tapa, villagers stripped bark from the paper mulberry tree. The gray outer coating of the bark was discarded and the white inner coating was peeled off in narrow strips. The bark was soaked in sea water, then pounded on a log until the narrow strips widened into ten-inch bands. The strips were overlapped and glued together with juice from the root of the manioc (cassava) plant to fashion large sheets of cloth.

METHODS OF DECORATING THE TAPA CLOTH INCLUDED OVERLAYING, CORD SNAPPING, PAINTING AND PRINTING. OVERLAYING WAS DONE BY PLACING A COLORED PIECE OF CLOTH OVER A PLAIN ONE AND BEATING THE TWO TOGETHER. IN CORD SNAPPING, A CORD DIPPED IN DYE WAS PLACED ON THE BARK, LIFTED IN THE MIDDLE AND ALLOWED TO SNAP BACK, PRODUCING A COLORED LINE. STAMPS FOR PRINTING WERE MADE FROM PIECES OF BAMBOO CARVED AT ONE END. THEY WERE DIPPED IN DYE AND PRESSED AGAINST THE CLOTH. MOST OF THESE DESIGNS WERE GEOMETRIC.

THE DYE COLORS, MADE FROM BERRY JUICES, WERE VARIOUS VALUES AND INTENSITIES OF BROWN AND REDDISH BROWN. BLACK WAS MADE FROM THE CANDLENUT TREE.

TAPA CLOTH WAS OFTEN SCENTED BY PLACING FRAGRANT PLANTS BETWEEN THE SHEETS OF CLOTH.

BROWN BAG IDEA

MATERIALS AND TOOLS

LARGE, PLAIN BROWN PAPER BAG

CRAYONS

WAX PAPER

SCISSORS

RULER

SINK OR LARGE BOWL OF WATER

IRON

DIRECTIONS

1. PREPARE THE PAPER BAG TO SIMULATE A CLOTH-LIKE TEXTURE BY SOAKING IT IN WATER FOR ABOUT TEN MINUTES. THIS LOOSENS THE GLUED SEAMS.

2. OPEN THE BAG AND CAREFULLY SQUEEZE OUT THE EXCESS WATER.

3. GENTLY SPREAD OUT THE BAG ON NEWSPAPER TO DRY. SOAKING AND CRUSHING THE PAPER, THEN SQUEEZING OUT THE WATER, WILL MAKE IT MORE PLIABLE. ANY TEARS THAT

OCCUR DURING THE PROCESS CAN BE MENDED ON THE BACK WITH TAPE AFTER THE PAPER HAS DRIED.

4. WHEN THE PAPER IS DRY, PLACE IT BETWEEN TWO PIECES OF WAX PAPER AND PRESS WITH A WARM IRON. (PROTECT THE IRONING SURFACE WITH NEWSPAPER.)

5. CUT THE DESIRED SIZE OF TAPA CLOTH FROM THE PREPARED PAPER.

6. PRACTICE MAKING A FEW SIMPLE GEOMETRIC DESIGNS ON A PIECE OF SCRAP PAPER. REFER TO THE EXAMPLES OF TRADITIONAL DESIGNS ON PAGE 137.

7. SELECT A SET OF DESIGNS YOU LIKE MOST AND ARRANGE THEM ON A PIECE OF PAPER THAT IS SIMILAR IN SIZE AND SHAPE TO YOUR PIECE OF PREPARED PAPER. REPEAT SOME DESIGNS TO CREATE A SENSE OF UNITY. DRAW THE DESIGNS ONTO THE PREPARED PAPER USING CRAYONS. USE A RULER FOR ACCURACY.

TAPA CLOTH DESIGNS

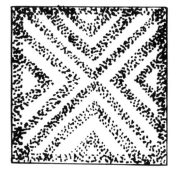

ACKNOWLEDGMENTS

MY SINCERE THANKS TO THE FOLLOWING PEOPLE, WHOSE CONTRIBUTIONS MADE THE WRITING OF THIS PUBLICATION POSSIBLE:

TO SONIA PLATA, STEADFAST FRIEND, FORMER STUDENT AND UNIVERSITY ASSISTANT. SONIA CONTRIBUTED SUPPORT IN COUNTLESS WAYS, FROM THE DAWN OF THE IDEA FOR THE BOOK THROUGH TO ITS COMPLETION.

TO WENDY JANISZEWSKI JAFFE, A FRIEND SINCE SHE WAS A MEMBER OF ONE OF MY ELEMENTARY ART CLASSES AT THE UNIVERSITY LABORATORY SCHOOL. YEARS LATER, AS A COLLEGE STUDENT, WENDY SET THE QUALITY AND STYLE OF THE ILLUSTRATIONS THROUGHOUT THIS BOOK.

TO KAY MORRISON, FOR HER ABILITY TO CONTINUE THE QUALITY OF WORK ESTABLISHED BY WENDY, AND FOR THE COMPLETION OF THE ILLUSTRATIONS.

TO LINDA ALVIRA, FOR HER CAPACITY TO UTILIZE THE COMPUTER IN PREPARING THE TEXT, AND FOR RENDERING AN ADDITIONAL SERIES OF DRAWINGS.

TO JEFFREY GALLATIN, LONGTIME FRIEND, FOR HIS ADVICE AND ENCOURAGEMENT, ESPECIALLY DURING THE EARLY STAGES OF THIS PROJECT.

TO MICHAEL HOUGH, FOR HIS PATIENCE AND CARE IN TAKING THE PHOTOGRAPHS.

TO PAULINE ROTHMEYER, J.D., FOR PREPARATION OF THE CONTRACT; TO ZANE OLUKALNS, FOR SECURING INFORMATION CONCERNING ISRAELI MOSAICS; AND TO BOTH, FOR THEIR SPECIAL INTEREST IN THE PUBLICATION.

TO MARTHA SIEGEL, FOR HER REMARKABLY CHEERFUL VOICE, CONSTANT ENCOURAGEMENT AND SOUND ADVICE WHENEVER I CALLED FEELING INTIMIDATED BY THIS VENTURE.

TO ALL OF MY FRIENDS AND FAMILY, WHO HAVE ENCOURAGED ME THROUGHOUT THIS UNDERTAKING, AND, LAST BUT FAR FROM LEAST, TO ALL OF THE STUDENTS FROM ELEMENTARY SCHOOL THROUGH GRADUATE LEVEL WHOM I HAVE HAD THE PRIVILEGE OF INSTRUCTING DURING MY FORTY-YEAR TEACHING CAREER. THE PLEASURE AND INSPIRATION GLEANED FROM WORKING WITH THESE ASPIRING ARTISTS PROVIDED THE STIMULUS AND MOTIVATION FOR THIS LITTLE VOLUME.